KISS YOUR Dragons

RADICAL RELATIONSHIPS, BOLD HEARTSETS, & CHANGING THE WORLD

Shawn Nason with Robin Glasco & Michael Harper

Kiss Your Dragons
Radical Relationships, Bold Heartsets, and Changing the World

By Shawn Nason with Robin Glasco and Michael Harper

Print: 978-1-944027-86-5
eBook: 978-1-944027-87-2

un/teaching    Networlding PUBLISHING

WARNING:

This is not a normal business book! You're about to begin a winding journey through a radical way of approaching your professional and personal life led by three dragon guides who aren't afraid to get real with each other and with you. This journey isn't for everyone, but if it's for you, strap on your armor, and let's go!

❝ *Let me not pray to be sheltered from dangers, but to be fearless in facing them. Let me not beg for the stilling of my pain, but for the heart to conquer it.* **❞**

—Rabindranath Tagore, *Collected Poems and Plays of Rabindranath Tagore*

Table of Contents

Chapter 1
Join Us on a Journey

It's no longer business as usual. It's now about bringing your awareness, values, and principles into the work you do—no matter where you are or how you're working.

We invite you to join us on an epic journey through this book. We'll show you how to create radical relationships that will move you from business mindsets into intuitive heartsets that will enable you to reach your goals, create changes you believe in, and live as a whole human being. We call it "living human."

Dragons play a starring role in our journey. Yeah, we're not even kidding here. The world needs you to embrace some cool sh*t about dragons. Are you up for it?

Most dragons are scary—at least the ones most Westerners know. Say "dragon" to the average Westerner and they think of Nordic warriors fighting a bunch of attacking dragons that are burning up villages and gobbling up slow-running villagers.

But in the Eastern world, the dragon is a powerful symbol—a benevolent, gracious, wise, helpful, and compassionate creature. In fact, dragons are so revered and worshiped in

China that they recognize nine different dragons that do everything from controlling time to helping with crops to defending the emperor. Shenlong, one of the nine dragons, even controls the wind, rainfall, and clouds.

For us, integrating East and West, the dragon represents the wisdom that sees the elemental reality of all situations. Frightening *and* protective, dragons are a powerful metaphor for the most difficult challenges, problems, fears, and possibilities that each of us faces each day.

And while many of us fear or run from our biggest challenges (dragons), they can also be viewed as wise protectors that are here to teach and help us. So why not have a more intimate relationship with them? Why not learn to kiss your dragons? What do you really have to lose?

A New Manifesto with Some Definitions

Kissing Your Dragons

We believe that rather than fight to keep all of life's challenges at bay, it's better to *embrace* them. That's what this book is about. And in embracing your challenges, you can use them like oxygen, like wings, like a powerful breeze that lifts you up over the world—to soar. *That's* what we mean by kissing your dragons. It's time to place a wet sloppy kiss on the things that are holding you back from being the you that the world needs you to be. Step in. Take some risks. Blow some sh*t up. When you do, your dragons will return power to you in the most unexpected ways.

Becoming a Dragon

In addition to kissing your dragons, we'll also be inviting you to channel the power and strength of a dragon. In this embodiment of dragon badassery, we're asking that you blow the sh*t out of this dragon metaphor and think bigger about breathing fire into your life and work. After all, whether or not you know it quite yet, you are a disruptor and the world needs you.

Radical Relationships

We'll show you how to kiss your dragons, but first you need to know that this isn't for the faint of heart. After all, even when they're helpful, dragons are some wild-ass beasts.

The starting place is all about relationships—radical relationships, to be more specific. When you're fortunate enough to have radical relationships, you can embrace *any* fear or challenge with wisdom, insight, humor, and greater awareness of yourself and those around you.

Like all healthy relationships, radical relationships are grounded in love and respect, but that's just the beginning. The radical part means busting down a wall or two and thinking more boldly about what it means to be in a relationship. An amazing example of this comes from a disruption sprint we led at Cure 4 the Kids Foundation in Las Vegas. During the sprint, their chief medical officer, our good friend Dr. Alan Ikeda, blew us all away. When we asked what value radical relationships could bring to Cure 4 the Kids in their mission to advance cures and prevention of childhood diseases, his simple, sobering response was, "Because we can't do this alone."

Boom. Mic drop. So much for doctors having egos, right?

Dr. Ikeda understands the power of breaking down the walls that have traditionally prevented relationships with people who could help him and his team save kids' lives. He understands the power of bringing in diverse voices who can offer a fresh—though sometimes messy—perspective. So who can help solve problems that Cure 4 the Kids faces each day? Well, bankers, for one. Fast food restaurant managers. Maybe throw in a real estate agent or two. Anyone with a different vantage point who is willing to engage in a meaningful relationship and stick it out when things get hard can put the "radical" into the relationship.

Radical relationships are about depth and authenticity, boldness and heart. More importantly, they're about being willing to be in relationships with people and systems that are very different from where you are and embracing the mess that comes with it.

This is about taking the time to sit with people you don't usually sit with. This is also about sitting in the mess even when every ounce of your being wants to run and hide. Done well, radical relationships give us confidence and energy in the face of ambiguity, confusion, difficulty, danger, and even despair. They build our trust in ourselves and in others. We need them now more than ever.

Rather than tell you what to do, we've created an adventure in the pages ahead to show you how to live differently through radical relationships *with* heartsets and mindsets. Taking it further, we want you in our swarm (more on that later). We also want to continue to be in relationship with you through our podcast and more. (For the record, there's no sales pitch here. There's nothing to buy. We just know the power of thinking radically about relationships and would love to be in a radical relationship with you.)

Mindsets

It's widely understood in the business world that your mindset shapes your opportunities. For example, a Google search for the word "mindset" produces no fewer than 175 million results.

Often defined as "the established set of attitudes held by someone," mindsets create our personal brands, drive our behaviors, and, if we're being honest, hold us back. In the more complex worlds of decision theory and general systems theory, a mindset is a set of assumptions, methods, or notions held by one or more people or groups of people. A mindset can also be seen as arising out of a person's worldview or philosophy of life.

We extend this meaning to include our ability as human beings to shift our thinking as we navigate the world around us and consider how we want to interact with other people.

Heartsets

Unless you're like the Tin Man in *The Wizard of Oz* before he was given the gift of a heart, you have a heart. But can your heart have an established set of assumptions, methods, and notions, like a mind? The answer, of course, is "yes." It's called a *heartset*.

Though the word "heartset" is much younger in its common usage than "mindset" (a Google search for "heartset" recently yielded just over four million results compared to the 175 million results from the word "mindset"), it's every bit as important. In fact, we believe heartsets are the missing link to better living and working. When we function exclusively from our heads and don't pay attention to our hearts, we're selling ourselves short and not living up to our potential.

One definition of heartset that's floating around out there is: "a deep-seated desire . . . a strong emotional connection with a person, place, or thing."[1] But we offer a different definition: acknowledging our heart's many truths that enable us to live a more positive, courageous life.

Combining Mindsets and Heartsets

By getting real about both our mindsets and our heartsets, we're able to significantly strengthen and radicalize our relationships. And why is this a priority? Because deep, authentic (radical) relationships are essential to both personal and business success and wellbeing.

Additionally, we fully believe that the world needs all of us to embrace a commitment to building radical relationships that make a difference. To this end, we're committed to empowering you to align your mindsets and heartsets. By doing so, you will create a powerful, fulfilling life and career for yourself and the people around you.

Mindsets	Heartsets
Falling in Love with the Problem	Kissing Your Dragons
Radical Relationships	Finding Your Dragon Swarm
A Bias toward Action	Unleashing Your Inner Fire
Show, Don't Tell	Being the Dragon
Do No Harm, Break Rules (Not Laws), and Proceed until Apprehended	Soaring with Your Dragons

Meet Your Dragon Guides

You'll be hearing our individual voices on the pages that follow, so allow us to introduce ourselves through the lens of runes. Leaning into the Nordic tradition that connects us to dragons, each of us has chosen a rune to symbolize our journey through this book with you. Often carved into small stones, runes are letters from an ancient Germanic alphabet that carry a deeper meaning. We'll explain each of our rune selections for you and then use them throughout the book to amplify our voices.

Shawn Nason

I'm the blow-it-up, mess-with-people, risk-taking natural big thinker. I'm what would happen if disruption and divergence had a baby. I've been working with leaders from all kinds of industries and backgrounds for three decades, and I've sometimes even been called a corporate pastor because I walk with people—all people—with an open heart and a commitment to telling the truth. I have no trouble being the bull in the china shop to get people thinking differently about the world around them.

My rune for this journey is Sowelu, which symbolizes wholeness and the energy of the sun. It speaks to self-understanding, the path that needs to be followed, and harnessing motivation through the uniqueness of one's soul. My connection to this rune challenges me to think holistically about this journey and teaches me to focus on the path that has been set before me.[2]

I'm a naturally creative thinker, master of metaphor and analogies, and somewhere in between Michael and Shawn on the disruption meter. To almost everyone that I meet, I'm the one who's way out there. I'm not afraid of thinking big and always interested in blowing sh*t up. But I tell ya, I met my match with Shawn because he's challenged me to embrace being uncomfortable, which has helped me get real and grow. He's definitely putting the radical in the relationship. Also, please feel free to call me "Khaleesi, Mother of Dragons."

My rune for this journey is Raido, which symbolizes the power of union and communication. It's grounded in bringing two sides together (righting the wrong) through a reliance on prayer, meditation, and paying attention to the inward and outward spirit. In connecting with this rune, I'm challenged to pay attention to what and who needs to be united and reunited on this journey. I also love that the concept of joy is embedded in this rune.[3]

Robin Glasco

Michael Harper

When it comes to risk, I'm pretty much the opposite of Shawn and not as bold as Robin. I used to think that I was a push-the-envelope kind of person until I started my disruption journey. Now I see that I'm the one who often starts with a "no" and overthinks pretty much everything. I mean, I won't apologize for thinking before I jump, but I also know that my life has been changed by these mindsets and heartsets. If you're reading this with any reluctance, though, you're definitely in my tribe.

My rune for this journey is Ehwaz, which symbolizes movement and progress, especially as they relate to improvement. It harnesses the commitment and energy needed to create change both within oneself and the world. As a learner on this journey with you, my connection to this rune provides peace of mind as we navigate a shifting landscape together.[4]

Chapter 2
Let's Talk about Dragons

Shawn: *Kiss Your Dragons*, the title of this book, is a metaphor, credo, and rallying cry we use to describe the unique, powerful, and equally crazy-hard journey it is to commit to creating positive change—always, everywhere, with everyone—in both work and life.

Think of your dragons as your trusted sidekicks who are strong, resilient, wise, and sometimes humorous, smart-ass guides who are constantly with you. They may be fearsome at first, but, as we pointed out earlier, they are benevolent creatures who will help you, even if they scare you. Your dragons can ride life's roller coaster with you and guide you through all the ups and downs that come your way.

With the support of your dragons, you will learn to embrace, practice, and eventually own a unique and powerful set of mindsets blended with heartsets. You will also learn to embody the power and strength that your dragons can give you.

Our dragon metaphor helps point us toward a more authentic, courageous life. Here are the key elements:

Balance
Fearlessness
Loyalty
Passion
Protection
Strength
Success
Wisdom

Robin: Dragons symbolize the ability to create immense possibilities. When the three of us work with leaders, this is usually our starting point, no matter what industry or what job, role, or level in the hierarchy of a company. Most of the people we work with are yearning for something new, but few are actually committed to jumping into the fire with us to create change. Too often, their hearts are looking for something bigger and newer, but their heads are filled with all of the barriers and pressures that are holding them back.

People who live in a place of possibility know that it's the very act of seeing and stating new opportunities that triggers resistance, fear, and doubt in both the explorer and the people around them. Do you want to create something new for yourself and your team? What about your friends and family?

We have a process for creating and living in radical relationships, and we're going to share it with you as openly as we can. It requires learning, embracing, and then practicing *five powerful mindsets* that move you to a whole new level of potential, and then doing the same with ***five life-altering heartsets***. Each of the five mindsets allows you to focus on how you think about the most important things in your life, including your family, your friends, your work, and the world. The five heartsets focus on what and how you feel when you trust your heart, your empathy, your caring, and your love for others. When you're able to use both, you can live from a new space of possibility.

 Shawn: There is a powerful Sioux legend that states:

The longest journey you will make in your life is from your head to your heart.

Having Native American heritage myself, I am honored by this time-tested advice. It describes and inspires our intention to connect the head and the heart.

Our message is simple: embrace the wonderful messiness of authenticity, relationships, and heart. That's our path, and we invite you to walk with us through this book.

Michael: Engaging your heart requires you to acknowledge and embrace your inner dragons. They're there, right? To connect with them, you have to start with some intentional, deep listening to others and yourself and make space for your discoveries to serve as truth finders and truth sayers. To be clear, this isn't the kind of listening that you do in the back of your head or while you're multitasking. We mean listening where you slow down, separate yourself from the rest of your reality, and really *hear* what the other person (or your own mind and heart) is telling you. It's basically "active listening" on steroids. The truths that you find when you listen this way will often lead you right to your dragons.

The kicker is that this type of listening is easier said than done. There are a million reasons to avoid it, from being too busy to being too afraid of hearing too much honesty, it's easy to make excuses for why you can't make time to do this kind of listening. Maybe the first dragon you need to make friends with is the reason why you're avoiding a deep listening session with yourself and others.

Once you listen, and only after you've listened, are you ready to move to co-creating. Co-creation is key to your individual and, when relevant, organizational success. For us, co-creating can evolve into facilitating, teaching, coaching, and actually walking alongside our client-partners (who throughout the rest of the book we'll simply call partners because that's how we feel about them).

Robin: Before we get too far into this journey together, you must first make a conscious choice with us to decide whether you're up for it. You have to decide whether you're more committed to living your life in a "business as usual" mindset or if you want to live an authentic life where you don't have to adopt a false identity to meet the needs of the situation or to accommodate others' expectations of you.

We are here to teach you *how* to kiss your dragons and then to do nothing short of *soar* with them. To help you on your quest we're sharing our stories—and having a conversation—a sometimes intimate and painful experience for us. Through the metaphor of dragons, we will help illuminate your path and create an adventure that will enrich not only your life but the lives of others you touch.

A Bit More about Heartsets

 Shawn: Since heartsets may be something new for you to think about, let's spend a few minutes helping you get more comfortable with them.

As Mahatma Gandhi said:

> Your beliefs become your thoughts.
> Your thoughts become your words.
> Your words become your actions.
> Your actions become your habits.
> Your habits become your values.
> Your values become your destiny.

Heartsets (beliefs) provide the core values that drive our behavior. They affect how we listen, how we think, and how we live and act. When we allow ourselves to travel from our minds to our hearts and stay there, where our values live, our words and deeds create unprecedented results. With all that is at stake in our world today, the way we show up in the world has never been of more critical importance. We face complex challenges each day and need to approach them with ready and focused hearts.

Embracing heartsets and kissing dragons go hand in hand. In the typical way we approach the world, we rationalize our decisions and then disguise any messiness or pain that results. Too many humans turn to unhealthy coping mechanisms (i.e., alcohol abuse, overeating, distancing ourselves from family members) instead of facing the "heart" of the issue. The act of kissing our dragons gets us out of our heads and into our hearts and challenges us to get honest about where life really happens.

Since you are reading this book, we know that like us, you are searching for something more, something better. At the time of this writing, we are in unprecedented times (COVID-19 pandemic) with daily disruptions that take us on emotional roller coaster rides. But you can have your wise and spirited advisors, your very own aides-de-camp—*your dragons*—at your side, in your mind and in your heart, minute by minute, day by day.

Heartsets are where your emotional intelligence shows up. Here you feel your clearest personal truths, in your heart. You might also feel something in your gut—your instincts. They will help you find the courage to show up for others, finding the truth in yourself and helping you to become a beacon for those around you.

Moving from mindsets to heartsets is a life-changing call to action. In fact, it's what the world, especially our business world, in our decades of experience doing transformation work, is begging for. Business leaders know that their very survival depends on how they are able to meet a future that is far from certain. You might also be personally aching for change in your own life. We certainly are.

While you move through the journey and the adventure of this book, you'll see firsthand how heartsets are even more important than mindsets because too often business leaders are unable or unwilling to engage their hearts. Of course, we're not saying that these folks are heartless. We're just saying that somewhere along the way, they learned to disengage their hearts and to stop paying attention to heartsets. We're here to change that.

Embracing Risks

 Shawn: By taking the bold step of writing and sharing this book with you, we're all taking a risk. We want to go further than we have gone before with our work.

Typical innovation lecturers yammer on about the fear of failure, of failing forward, or failing back, or failing cheaply. I'm sick and tired of hearing those things. I don't want to talk about it anymore. It's bullsh*t and I'm bored. And I work in innovation! I don't want to talk about that anymore, because what have we accomplished with that approach? Nothing! What has drastically changed in innovation in the last ten years? Nothing!

This is often what happens to chief innovation officers. They start off strong in an organization with lots of enthusiasm and support, and within two years they're ready to leave. That's the pattern. Or they stay and the innovation-forward CEO leaves and all the good work goes out the window. So, let's address the heart issues and the heartsets, and let's do it right now. To me, failure is tied to risk. How much risk are you willing to take? How bold is your ambition?

I live every day knowing I could lose everything. I'm OK if that should include losing my job. The day that I told Robin she needed to resign from her innovation job at a major insurance provider, she broke out into a sweat and had to sit down, and I had to talk her off a metaphorical ledge. We have different approaches, feelings, mindsets, and heartsets about risk—including financial risks, security risks, and entrepreneurship risks.

 Robin: Yep. Every day for two or three months straight, I broke out into a cold sweat.

Shawn: But I kept saying, "Robin, you need to move on to something else. You're miserable right now. It's time." But she would reply, "I can't, Shawn. I have two kids in college. I have this 401(k). I have to have a certain salary to move forward. I have to keep at this and make it work."

Then I responded, "OK, so go ahead and be unhappy. But the best thing you can do for yourself is to . . . *quit your job!*" I continued to nudge her about it during the next few months.

Fast-forward three months. My phone rang at 6:00 a.m. and it was Robin. She said matter-of-factly, "I wrote my letter and today I'm going in to tell my boss that I quit." I responded with a simple, "It's about f*cking time."

Robin: I remember a lot of time spent on the phone with Shawn during that time. We probably talked at least once a day before I quit. And then after I quit, we probably talked about four times a day!

Shawn: Yeah, because after she turned in her resignation, risk and anxiety kicked in. She would complain regularly, "I don't have a job. What am I going to do? I'm going to be homeless!" I assured her she would not be homeless.

Robin: I remember everything about the day I quit: what I wore, who I spoke with, what I said—everything about that day. And this is significant because my memory is not the best. I'm the elder stateswoman in this group, and my memory is horrible. But a pivotal moment like that stuck like glue to me. I was more of a "do what I say not what I do" person.

But now, because of Shawn and his constant support, walking beside me, I was able to lean in, feel the fear, but still take the risk.

 Shawn: The important thing with her example is that we annihilated the big stuff in Robin's life instead of getting caught up in the small stuff, and in doing so made all the difference for her moving forward. And her risk paid off.

Something similar happened with Michael. We first had a working relationship when he worked for a vendor I used at a previous job. Over time, as our relationship developed, I saw his many talents. At that time, I was traveling to where he lived in Kentucky and we forged a friendship through our business relationship. I was always looking for someone to have dinner with and he was always down for some Mexican food at our favorite restaurant. Remember, Michael? I told you for almost two years, "We're going to work together." And Michael's answer was. . . .

 Michael: Hell, no! Not ever. It'll never happen.

 Shawn: Michael now runs MOFI (our strategy/design SWAT team) for me. He's thriving in the number-two spot, as is our company. This is what building radical relationships is all about. We're very different people, but we've leaned into our differences, kissed our dragons, and challenged each other to see things from different perspectives.

Michael: Let's be honest here, though. You and I have a very different understanding of risk.

Shawn: That's so true, Michael. As a risk-averse type of person, you prefer to play it safe and always have a backup plan. I swing for the fences.

For instance, we laugh because Michael will put a few dollars in a slot machine and feel like the world is coming to an end; I'll put, well, let's just say much, much more than that on a craps table and not think twice about it.

A few dollars is how he responds to the uncertainty of winning and the possibility of losing because $10 is $10 to him. Me? Having $10 on the table means an opportunity to risk that money to create a bigger payout because I live in risk and think nothing about failure. So, is it fear of failure, or is it the fear of leaning into risk? He's happy to get a lower payout for lower risk. I prefer the higher potential payoff in exchange for a bigger risk.

 Michael: Risk is fine if you're a risk taker. I'm not a big risk taker because my whole identity is based on being the stable, everything-is-fine, responsible one. There's no right, wrong, good, or bad here, but to truly lean into kissing your dragons, you do need to take steps to embrace some risk in your life. Or, at the very least, start moving away from always starting with a "no" mindset (as hard as it might feel) and start being open to the possibilities that are all around you.

I'm wired that way. I don't know how much is nature versus nurture, but I was raised in a family where you didn't spend money. The "you have to spend money to make money" mindset didn't exist.

Robin: I aways have to factor public judgment into people's level of risk tolerance. That's part of our mission to help people get real.

It's time to stop looking at, believing in, and caring about what other people are saying about you and focus on your heart, your desires, and who you are and what you're comfortable with. You may (or may not) need to challenge yourself to move out of your comfort zone, but that's your decision, not the world's.

Shawn: This goes back to the difference between a heartset and a mindset. Your heartset holds your values, how you live and work. Every day that Michael works with me, he has to challenge his personal value system to live in this space. We're good for each other—that's the joy of radical relationships. They support us, but they push us too. They help us grow even when they feel uncomfortable.

Michael: Yes. What he said is true. And it's also important to learn to be OK with being uncomfortable. We grow when we're stretched. That's exactly what happens in the gym: working out creates these little microtears in your muscles, then the muscle fibers heal and come back thicker and stronger. Then (if you keep going) you do it again. Discomfort isn't a bad thing. It actually teaches you that something is happening inside of you. If you pay attention, you'll see that the change in you is good!

Shawn: And to me, that discomfort is more than just fear of failure. It's about pushing into it further, being willing to lose it all at any moment. I thrive on the feeling that comes with risk. It charges me up!

Michael: When you say, "lose it all," I think "lose" is relative. It depends on how big the risk is, how big the bet is. What is a risk to me would bore Shawn. What's a regular risk to Shawn might completely paralyze me. So, it's important for all of us to understand that at some point we all feel the pain of risk, but we all have a different tolerance for that pain.

The sheer nature of human beings is to have a ton of different things, including risks, going on daily. I've always been the one who makes the safe choices and gets rewarded for them. Personally, when I have done things that are risky, I have not been rewarded. So, what do you think I'd most naturally stick with? And, by the way, my life is great. I've got an amazing family, I have all the resources I need to have a fulfilled life. And I've never had a job I didn't like. Not being a risk taker doesn't mean you're a coward or a loser. It just means you're not naturally a risk taker and you may have to work a little harder when you're embracing radical relationships.

Are You Ready?

Robin: Heartsets. Mindsets. Dragons. Risk. If you're still with us, you're in for one hell of a journey. We're here to teach the *why* of what you can do along with the *how* so that you can do a better job of actually making sh*t happen and learning how to soar!

And, for us, it all comes back to building radical relationships in your life. When your heart and mind are aligned and you put some radical into your relationships, you'll create and co-create new opportunities and possibilities that will change your life. And, in changing your life, you will change the lives of the people around you on your way to changing the world.

Ultimately, when you walk with and then learn to soar with your dragons through radical relationships, we believe you will make a difference that matters in a world ripe for bold new ideas and brave souls.

Michael: So, let us tell you our shared story, which is filled with so many smaller stories that we could never record all of them in a book.

We invite you into our radical relationships with each other, our friends and family, and our partners (disguised to protect the innocent!). Join us on an adventure that we know will help you build not only a better work-life, but also a better whole life.

We want you to experience the feeling of connection, camaraderie, and heart that we have for one another, for our partners, our family, and you. We hope through our dialogues in this book you feel like you are right beside us. You are already part of our community. You are essential to making this book come to life!

If you are reading these words, this is exactly where you should be. We are confident that, just like our three journeys brought us together in unlikely ways, there is a reason that you are connecting your journey to ours by engaging this book.

But, the question remains, are you ready for this sh*t?

Summary

Kiss Your Dragons is a metaphor, credo, and rallying cry we use to describe the unique, powerful, and equally crazy-hard journey it is to commit to creating positive change—always, everywhere, with everyone—in both work and life.

Heartsets (beliefs) provide the core values that drive our behavior. They affect how we listen, how we think, and how we live and act. When we allow ourselves to travel from our minds to our hearts and stay there, where our values live, our words and deeds create unprecedented results.

In this journey through the five mindsets and heartsets, you will experience all the messiness and risk of radical relationships. By embracing the mess and leaning into the risk, you will discover a new way of seeing the world.

Chapter 3
Getting Radical

Shawn: Now that you understand the basics of radical relationships, it's time to drill down a bit and give you a chance to connect them to your life.

Radical relationships happen between people and communities that may appear to have little in common. The conversations that happen are raw, real, authentic, and transparent. To engage, you have to first understand that the other person or people are holding onto something that you need to learn or experience. And you have to be fully open to changing your mindsets, heartsets, values, and behaviors based on what you learn or experience.

I live every day ready to have conversations, which form the core of these relationships. Why? Why do some people call me a "corporate pastor?" It goes back to heartsets.

When I was growing up, my mother slept with a police scanner next to her bed. If there was a fire in our community, or a single mom was out of a place to stay, or anyone was in need, she would learn about it through the police scanner. Several times in my childhood, I heard my mother get up in the middle of the night, get in her car, and head to a scene of an accident or a fire to help take care of the affected people. Sleeping with a police scanner nearby has little to do with a mindset. In fact, it doesn't make a ton of sense when you think about it. But, if you look at it through the lens of a heartset (caring for people in need), it makes all the sense in the world.

Even when I'm exhausted and don't feel like doing anything, I still make myself lean into the heartsets that drive me towards radical relationships in my life because I believe it's what the world needs most right now. If all of us put each other first, we would create a completely different world.

To have radical relationships you have to have honesty, integrity, trust, and loyalty.

As Michael will tell you, I live by these standards and expect others to live by them, too. They are the foundation to changing the world through thinking differently about relationships. It takes all of these lofty words working together to make a radical relationship come alive and get to the depth and breadth that needs to happen for actual change to take place.

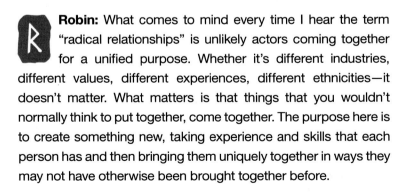 **Robin:** What comes to mind every time I hear the term "radical relationships" is unlikely actors coming together for a unified purpose. Whether it's different industries, different values, different experiences, different ethnicities—it doesn't matter. What matters is that things that you wouldn't normally think to put together, come together. The purpose here is to create something new, taking experience and skills that each person has and then bringing them uniquely together in ways they may not have otherwise been brought together before.

Shawn: I don't believe there has to be a purpose in a radical relationship. It can just exist, which drives Michael nuts. It's not uncommon for Michael to give me a warning on our way to business meetings or social events by saying, "We cannot collect any best friends today, Shawn."

I create radical relationships just to have them, and to know that at some point for me a radical relationship may end up changing my life in a big or small way.

Michael: I have a complicated relationship with radical relationships. (There I said it.) If you're reading along and scratching your head a bit, I get it. Shawn and Robin lean into relationships much more easily than I do. I'm a total extrovert, I know how to light up a room, and I need to be around people as much as possible or I'll implode. But, when it comes to investing time developing real relationships with people outside my family, I'd much rather invest my time in my work to get sh*t done and make big things happen. And let's be clear, I excel at getting sh*t done and making big things happen quickly without sacrificing excellence.

If we're being honest, when Shawn and Robin start talking about relationships and especially radical relationships, I get a knot in the pit of my stomach because I know what it means.

When I first started on this journey with Shawn, the knot in my stomach came from knowing that, instead of keeping things simple and controllable, we were going to add more variables to the situation and waste time getting to know people. It meant going down the path of hanging out (instead of getting work done) and making things harder by bringing more voices into the conversation, which just makes everything messier. In short, it meant making my life and work harder. (Thanks for nothing, Shawn.)

As I've struggled to embrace the power of radical relationships, I still get a knot in my stomach, but it's for different reasons. The knot comes from knowing that my life and work will be harder, but it's the right thing to do. I know it will take physical, mental, and spiritual energy to make a radical relationship happen. I know that I have to intentionally set aside my preference to stay in control and deal with the dragons that are preventing me from stepping into the relationships. In short, it's the opposite of what I would naturally do, it will take a ton of work, and my life will be better for it. (Thanks for everything, Shawn.)

So, for people like me, and especially people in the business world who either don't have time for relationships or think that's just not their jam, that's OK. Radical relationships don't come naturally to everyone. However, that's not an excuse for avoiding them. Get your sh*t together, figure out what's holding you back, and get ready for a life-changing journey. It won't be easy, but you won't regret it.

Thinking Bigger

Shawn: It's time to start thinking differently—thinking bigger—about your relationships in both life and work. My purpose in life is to live in radical relationships, to dive into deep personal connections with people rather than being satisfied with surface connections. This is why I don't mind being called a corporate pastor. I'm on call twenty-four hours a day. It's not uncommon for me to have 20-plus phone calls each day, and more often than not, they begin in the wee hours of the morning because people know that I'll pick up the phone. That's the pastor in me. I sleep—just as my mother did—with my phone next to me, and I'll answer it 24/7.

When COVID-19 started, I struggled because we were used to holding in-person design sprints to make stuff happen. Using the metaphor of a church service, I get up and I give what you could call the sermon, and I give the altar call. Robin takes the offering, and Michael runs Sunday school. We joke about it, but I don't know any other way to explain it.

The thing about my message (sermon) is that it doesn't change. This is something that Michael has told me many times blows him away. My message is simple and has just three points:

Be transparent, build relationships, and love people.

I may deliver that sermon three times in the same day, but I "preach" it in a different way, and that's what people have come to expect from me.

As a boy, I was steeped in sermons. I grew up in a Southern Baptist home, but—surprise, surprise—guess who got bored in that church? Me. It was way too calm and way too predictable to hold my interest.

So, I went out and found one of the first big megachurches in the country in the early 1980s. As a result, you could say that musically I'm a little bit of a mixture of Jerry Lee Lewis, Mickey Gilley, and Jimmy Swaggart. I have rockabilly in my soul that comes out in lots of different, creative ways.

For example, when I was 13 years old, I just sat down and started playing the piano. I was that kid who never needed a lesson and never really had to practice much, but still managed to win every competition I entered. But when I play, I beat the hell out of the piano. (Michael is more of a traditional, trained pianist, and that's how he describes my technique!) That's the rockabilly flowing through me that is evident in how I approach a keyboard and how I live my life.

As I mentioned, Robin does the offering portion of our session. She knows how to tug at people's heartstrings, which is the pathway to their purse strings. She's the mom of our group. She can get up and say, "We need to raise $500,000 for Little Jimmy," and she will raise $750,000. Only in her case, she's not raising money for Little Jimmy—she's inspiring teams to kiss their dragons and move forward and claim their success. All three of us approach radical relationships differently, but all of the relationships are still radical.

Michael: Radical relationships are also important because of the amount of trust and influence that comes with them. Though it's best to enter these relationships with no specific intention beyond seeing what could come of it, for me it's important to claim that, when you walk alongside people, something happens. I'm going to call it influence instead of change, but you could also make an argument for change.

I started working with Shawn in earnest in June 2018, but I didn't give up my other business until seven months later. Remember, my response to his offer to join his business was a very strong "hell no." So, it was a full seven months doing multiple jobs. Even though he wanted me to join his team, I wasn't ready to make the leap into a startup with all the risk that comes with it.

On a car ride with Shawn at one point during those months, I looked at him and said, "Give me a date." I wanted him to give me a deadline for needing to piss or get off the pot. His response? A big fat "Hell no. You have to figure this out on your own, and I'm going to give you all the time you need to do it."

The truth is, I wanted someone else to make the decision for me so I wasn't on the hook if it didn't work out. Deep down, I wanted to be able to blame someone else if it turned out to be the wrong decision.

After a few more weeks of spinning and overthinking, I decided that I was going have to give myself a deadline for making a decision, so I went with January 1, 2019. It was time. I couldn't keep up multiple commitments any longer. I had a conversation with my wife (who is much smarter than me) about whether she'd be OK with me taking such a big career risk. She encouraged me to make the jump, but I still wasn't ready. I could still think of a million reasons why taking this risk was a bad idea. Luckily, I had a few more weeks before my self-imposed deadline.

As it turns out, we were going to Puerto Rico for New Year's. As my deadline approached, I did my best to make excuses for why I wasn't going to be able to make a decision. As much as I tried to ignore the pressure, it kept bubbling up.

One day in Old San Juan, the pressure got to be too much so I made myself go for a walk and—as scary as it was—I committed to spend time thinking through how I was going to move forward in the new year. I walked along a wall that overlooked the ocean and experienced a range of emotions as I remembered all of the intense adventures that I'd had living into the mindsets and heartsets that Shawn was showing me. But was this how I wanted to continue living and working? Was I going to take the safe, easy choice or was I going to make the leap and try something new? I knew that I couldn't continue living with one foot in the adventure and the other foot in the safety zone.

Then, it started to rain. And I didn't have an umbrella.

Now, to some of you, being caught in the rain would be no big deal. For me, though, it was a complete failure and I felt like a loser. I should have thought ahead and prepared for possible rain; after all, it was an overcast day and thinking ahead is my jam. All I could think about was how desperately I wanted my raincoat so I could enjoy the rest of my walk. Without it, there's no way that I could be happy.

Then it hit me like a ton of bricks. Why do I always focus on what I don't have instead of paying attention to the opportunities in front of me? It took some effort, but I pushed the negative thoughts about my lack of preparation out of my head, which allowed me to start seeing the life and beauty all around me. My perspective changed.

That's when it became clear that I needed to accept Shawn's offer and take the risk. What if I pushed the negatives out of my head and heart so I could focus on the opportunity ahead of me? What if I could learn to enjoy the messy and painful times as much as the funny and inspirational moments? The more I walked, the more I knew I was going to be OK. I was ready to ride the roller coaster with 100 percent of my energy and to start seeing the messiness as an opportunity to grow. I knew that I couldn't do it halfway. If I was going to jump, I had to be all-in and not let myself complain when things got hard.

That rain became a cleansing experience for me. I walked and leaned into the path ahead of me instead of obsessing about everything that could go wrong around me. The decision was made. And do you want to guess what appeared in the sky as the rain ended and my walk was complete? Yep, a rainbow. You can't make this sh*t up, right?

I guess you could say that this was the moment where I quit trying to fight one of my dragons and instead figured out a way to give it a big kiss on the nose. Getting caught in the rain may not seem like a lot to some of you, but to me, it was a life-changing moment. It was also a reminder of the power of radical relationships.

Blurring the Lines

 Shawn: That's a powerful story, Michael, that captures the life-changing nature of what we're talking about here.

Remember, there doesn't have to be a purpose in radical relationships. Going back to how Michael repeatedly tells me, "We can't collect any more best friends today, Shawn," I'm building radical relationships just to have them. And radical relationships aren't reserved just for the workplace. They carry into our personal lives and many times the personal relationships are even more important than the professional ones. It's all about building vibrant and sustainable exchanges.

This blurry line between personal and professional relationships is often startling to people who aren't used to it, especially people who are used to a corporate environment. It's more authenticity than some folks are willing to handle and it means blowing up the office norms that so many people have come to accept. To me, it's just more of what needs to be blown up so that we can actually move forward and make sh*t happen in the world.

I'm just sick and tired of organizational cultures where people feel the need to put up walls to protect themselves and get ahead instead of focusing on the consumer and what's best for the entire team. I'm tired of the fear and pettiness that comes from grown-ass adults who feel stuck in cultures that suck the life out of them. And most of all, I'm done with complacent leaders who do things the same old way because that's the way it's always been done.

Melding personal and professional relationships isn't always easy—in fact, it's downright messy at times—and the mess is just part of the process. Embracing the mess leads to people who are more passionate, capable, and fully present in both their personal lives and their work. By stepping into authentic relationships where people feel like they can truly be themselves, we unlock a whole new level of inspiration and productivity.

And every time something new emerges for any of us, we respect each person's opinion and process.

Robin: I definitely agree that success happens through relationships. Great relationships, radical relationships, are with the people who will fight for you, who you want to fight alongside. I just see good things happening from that. You don't need to worry about what these relationships may look like at the beginning or what they might evolve into. You're letting go of outcomes, which allow for lots of possibilities.

I view the world through a problem lens, not from a pessimistic one. I definitely get accused of being more optimistic than pessimistic. I'm OK with that. But it's more so with my disruptor hat on: falling in love with the problem, saying something like,

"Wow! Wouldn't it be great to solve this for humankind?"

Shawn: The reason Robin turned projects over to me when she worked at her previous job was because in our radical relationship, we had built a trust bank. At

some point in a relationship, you're going to need to cash a check when you mess up. At that moment you better have enough relationship collateral deposited in your trust bank.

A prime example happened just the other day. We had fallen behind a little bit with some deliverables because of a miscommunication issue. This kind of situation is inevitable in the business world and the differentiator is how we respond to it, right? Because Michael Harper, Shawn Nason, and Robin Glasco had a trust bank with the core team there, we were able to make a withdrawal and say, "Hey, we messed up and here's how we're going to make it right." Because of that trust bank, our relationship didn't suffer. In fact, it got stronger.

Michael: Yes, and as you might imagine, we build trust differently than a lot of other folks. And not to be a broken record here, but as you might also imagine, we build trust through these radical relationships, which includes blurring these lines between personal and professional. And that's not easy.

I've only been on this journey with Shawn for a couple of years and I'm definitely still learning these mindsets and heartsets. Because of this, I can empathize with the majority of our partners (and likely some of you) who often have some difficulty shifting their attention and commitment to learning what Shawn and the rest of our team are here to teach, coach, and nurture.

In other words, it's damn hard to learn, embrace, and practice the five mindsets-to-heartsets we are sharing in this book. It's damn hard to fully embrace the ups and downs of radical relationships. And, let's face it—it's just damn hard to change sometimes, especially if you're trying to make significant changes without the help of a community around you to support you.

As we warned at the beginning of this book, this journey isn't for everyone. But, for those who are ready and willing, this journey can turn into a life-changing experience that can create a much more fulfilling professional and personal life.

Summary

Embracing radical relationships means thinking differently (bigger) about your relationships in both life and work and embracing the messiness that comes with it. This isn't about trying to work on your relationships a little bit. This is about stretching yourself to completely rethink how you approach and interact with the world around you.

Though radical relationships may vary in terms of depth and impact, it's important to remember that these relationships don't have to have a purpose. It's OK to have relationships just for the sake of having them and then being open to how the relationships affect you in small or significant ways.

Jumping into this way of living and working means getting messy. Embracing the messiness is part of existing more authentically and getting real about the bullsh*t that surrounds you. It's not always the easiest path to take, but it will often be the most fulfilling.

Chapter 4

Falling in Love with the Problem and Kissing Your Dragons

Robin: Think for a moment about the meanest, angriest dragon you can possibly imagine. No, really. Close your eyes and picture it in your head. How do the dragon's looks, smells, and sounds strike terror in you and everyone around you?

If you were to come face-to-face with this monster, what might you be thinking and saying? Most likely, you'd be thinking how to avoid being burned, killed, and/or eaten, right? You might even say things like,

"Someone (not you) needs to fight it!"

"We need to make sure that dragon is put in a cage."

"We must stop that dragon from getting out among the people."

"We need to slay this dragon immediately!"

What do these statements have in common? They focus on solutions instead of the problem. More specifically, they focus on fear-based solutions instead of the problem.

This is perhaps the most challenging concept you'll need to understand. Don't make the leap from fear to solution without examining and understanding the problem.

Your goal? Fall in love with your dragons before considering your solutions.

Yeah. We know. It's really, really hard to fall in love with something that looks like it could take your head off before it has its first cup of morning coffee. But it can be done.

- Do you exist in a culture where it takes a long time to get things done?

- Do you find yourself making only incremental adjustments rather than committing to necessary, but uncomfortable, significant improvements?

- Do you have solutions that you are finding tough to sell or present to new customers?

These situations are most likely symptoms that you're falling in love with your solutions, putting them first over first falling in love with your problems. This is a costly mistake. Why?

I don't really care what the problem is per se. It's more about making sure you're solving the *right problem*. As a wise person once said, "We too often solve the wrong problem—precisely." We humans can't help but fall in love with solutions. We are solution-focused creatures.

But what we need to realize is that it's our challenges that hold the keys to creating deep, genuine, long-term relationships that lead us to solving our problems. These radical relationships are essential to both our work and lives beyond the workplace.

Why can't we approach every challenge with the intention to be creative? I've always talked about everyone's ability to be a disruptor and how we all can be creative. People say things to me all the time like, "I'm not bold," "I'm not creative," or "I'm not a risk taker."

When our partners are mired in challenges, we do our best to help them take one step at a time toward reaching their goals. My direction to them is, "You *can* get there from here," in any part of your life. There will be a doorway or a window that you can open simply by taking a risk and being innovative. In fact, you can open doors and windows that you didn't even realize existed prior to taking that risk.

My intent is to inspire others to take a look around at the biggest problems (aka dragons) and think, "This is something other people in my company do *now*, so if they can do it, so can I." If I can accomplish that goal, then I feel great.

Once you help others start their journey, they discover their potential to open a new door to new possibilities. Then as you help them they start to realize they are building a positive momentum toward their goals.

I'm an extremely visual person, so I like to give analogies based on movies or TV shows. One of my favorite movies is *The Shawshank Redemption*. Now, I'm not a big prison movie person, but I'm attracted to the story that takes place between Red (Morgan Freeman) and Andy (Tim Robbins). Andy is an innocent man who has been sent to prison, and I love his evolution throughout the film. I'm also a big fan of a surprise ending when it's handed to me.

I'm paraphrasing a bit here, but one of the lines I love is when Andy asks Red, "Hey, remember that place—would you be willing to come join me?" With these words, Andy sets forth an offer to reconnect in a beautiful setting where we've come to learn there's a tin container buried under a rock wall. When Red gets out of jail and finally makes it to put his hands on the tin can, he finds a note that says, "If you've come this far, maybe you'd be willing to go a little further." It's the steady encouraging cryptic words provided by Andy that Red uses to keep going during the years of imprisonment to eventually rendezvous at their prearranged tropical paradise.

That beautiful reconnection Andy and Red experience reminds me of my parents who, when trying to teach my siblings and me how to swim, didn't just throw us in the deep end without warning. Instead, they slowly coaxed us to take one step and then another. "Let's just put our toes in," they'd say as they eased us into going a little further. "OK, now lift your legs a bit. Now splash lightly with your arms. OK, now get a little water on your face." It's a step-by-step approach.

Or another analogy might be how former NFL player-turned-actor Terry Crews shares how he moves from hating working out to committing to working out regularly. This comes from a man who is known for being able to literally make his pecs "dance."

He is incredibly built, yet he hates to work out. So he talks about starting the process with, "I'll just put on my workout clothes. Then I'll just drive to the gym. Once I'm there, I think to myself, 'I'm dressed, I might as well go in.' And then once I go in, what am I gonna do, just stand there? I've gotta do something!"

I share this because his strategy for self-motivation about a fitness routine illustrates so well how to break up anything you hate or dislike doing into small chunks. This is the best way to create behavioral change. By making something a habit, it's easier to continue to build upon that habit stepwise, making it easy to do. It's about shifting your attitude a bit about what you're doing anyway. Instead of putting on your suit, put on some workout clothes. You have to get dressed anyway.

Every step you take, another iterative opportunity arises or another door opens up. There may actually be many doors, so you keep going. When working with someone who's terrified of change or risk-taking, you can help them along by simply saying, "Hey, wherever you are, think of it this way: every step could open a door. Be looking for the doorway. Something good is going to happen."

People are not afraid of changes that they believe are in their best interest. People resist change because deep inside there's something about the change they believe, suspect, or feel is not in their best interest. Even people who claim to hate change will not resist if they see something or decide the change is good for them. Give yourself the opportunity to see that change benefits you and it's OK to take some small steps (risks) to get you moving forward.

When I worked in a large organization, I loved having fun with my out-of-office email message when I took time off. I would say cute things like, "Hey, I'm out. And there's a funny thing about my email—it likes to be left alone when I'm gone so I'll connect with you when I get back." I loved putting a little bit in there about where I was heading and what I might do while I was there. People would always say, "Where are you going next? I just can't wait to see what you write." But most people would just sigh and say, "I wish I could do that."

When pressed for an explanation of what was preventing them from having some fun with something as simple as an out-of-office message, they'd tell me they were afraid their boss would say that it wasn't appropriate or that they would be seen as unprofessional. Over time, I'd coax them into joining me in having some fun with their out-of-office message. I'd gotten the ball rolling for them by showing them that it's possible to do it and not get fired. I'd help them write something simple and fun. They'd take a deep breath, give it a whirl, and then realize that they still had a job. Never underestimate the power of taking a small risk by following in someone's footsteps.

Moving into a place where you can kiss your dragons means knowing that there are people who can help you on your journey. When you watch for those people, you will find them and they will give you the courage to take another step and then another.

Do You Fall in Love with Problems or Solutions?

Shawn: To me, falling in love with the problem means annihilating the big stuff and ignoring the little stuff. Focus on solving *big problems*. Just *go*! Blow them up. Don't worry about the little stuff. It's not about focusing on the low-hanging fruit. Lots of people are easily distracted by the little problems on the ground that seem easier to address. They just bend over and pick them up. They're half-rotted, anyway. Going for the big problems, though, means confronting the dragons that were distracting you by focusing your attention on the easier, rotten stuff. What about those bigger problems scares you or makes you think you can't blow them up?

Robin: Agreed. Good call-out. We've all been there, done that. But now, we're here to encourage you to grab the fruit at the top. Don't just take the easy route and pick it off the low-hanging branches or off the ground. What we're challenging ourselves, and you, to do is to think about how to reach a little further. Sometimes you can't clearly see it. But go ahead and grab that stuff that's on the top of the tree. Get someone to give you a leg up. Reach for it, pluck it, stare fear in the face, and then breathe some fire into it!

Ultimately you're going to have to do it anyway, so rather than continuing to gather up the old easy pickings, let's just go ahead and grab for the hardest to reach, but the most important.

Shawn: Yeah. I'm not spending my career right now just to make things a little bit better. I want to annihilate the sh*t out of entire systems and rebuild them correctly with the right people in the room.

Robin: That's Shawn! Most people view problems using their existing resources. Shawn clearly doesn't. This is why, in our teachings, we focus differently on the idea of resources. This can be illustrated by one of my favorite scenes from *Apollo 13*. In the movie (which is based on the true story), after a life-threatening explosion on the spacecraft while in space, the support team on the ground had to figure out how to get the astronauts safely back to earth. At one point, the carbon dioxide level on the spacecraft was rising to a dangerous level. So, a group of engineers poured out a box of supplies they knew the crew had on board and figured out how to use those limited resources in creative ways to make a carbon dioxide scrubber and save the lives of the astronauts.

Through their deep belief that a solution was possible, they sifted and sorted, looking for something that was, prior to this point, used for a totally different purpose. They finally found some unique, disparate parts that they could hack to save the ship and, more importantly, the astronauts' lives.

So just like NASA engineers, you have all the assets and resources that you will need to find your dragons, name them, connect with them, and then soar with them. However, you will likely need to think about your assets and resources differently. You will need to reimagine, reexamine, and give the middle finger to the rules and then break through to a new and better product, business, and life!

We're normally taught to go for the low-hanging fruit or that which has fallen on the ground. We're saying, "No. Screw that! Find some big-ass dragons and, rather than slay them, kiss them!" It can be done, and we will show you how.

To be more specific, we're talking about metaphorically addressing your fears, especially what we see in so many of our partners: *the fear of public failure.* Yes, private failures that get under your skin and cause anxiety can be a problem. When you're in the quiet moments within yourself and inside your own mind, you often hear shouts from your critic-corner slither forth when you fail in some way.

But when your failure is on your main stage with a large headline, that's not a comfortable place. Failure has long been implanted in our brains, It's the big "F." It's the incomplete, it's the "You came in last place," it's the "You didn't _____" (fill in the blank here). There's a lot of discussion in the business world about embracing failure. In our experience, most of it is just talk. Our goal here in this book is to help you do a 180 in how you view failure.

A Dragon Encounter

Shawn: Let's dive into an amazing animated movie series about dragons called *How to Train Your Dragon* that takes falling in love with your problem to a whole new level. Here, the main character, Hiccup Horrendous Haddock III, a tenacious young Viking boy, befriends an unlikely playmate, a dragon he names Toothless.

(Fun fact: It's Viking tradition to call the runt of the litter a "hiccup." In these movies, Hiccup seems to have gotten his name from the fact that he was born early, so he was smaller and weaker than the other babies.)

Hiccup is the Viking son to the king of the clan and therefore he is heir to the throne. But we learn early on in the movie that he's much different than the other Vikings in the village. Not only is he scrawnier than the other young people around him, he also thinks differently.

Although Hiccup is willing to assume the risk of fighting the dragons who attack his village and even has engineered some creative ways to fight, he has a transformational experience when he encounters a wounded dragon that he ends up naming Toothless. Instead of seeing a dangerous archenemy in this dragon, he sees a defenseless soul thrashing around in pain and misery with a broken tail, which makes it impossible for him to fly. Toothless the dragon needs Hiccup the weak Viking boy to survive.

In a rare, brave move, Hiccup not only saves the dragon's life, but befriends him. This is the epitome of kissing a dragon. Think about this for a moment in terms of your personal and professional life. We have always been conditioned to look at dragons as harmful, sometimes even evil. But like the Chinese dragon culture, let's see our dragons as legendary creatures that symbolize success, loyalty, fearlessness, strength, balance, and immense possibilities.

In innovation, all of these elements are in play with consumers, particularly when you talk about the front end of innovation (ideation). In the ideation process, you have to be fearless; you have to show strength. You have to show possibilities when nobody else is seeing the possibilities. Having a dragon as your guide means that you are fierce and confident in everything you do. But it also means that as fierce and scary as you can be sometimes, ultimately your sole purpose is always to befriend and benefit people.

Engaging Your Dragons

Shawn: Engaging your dragons means thinking about all of those troubling thoughts that can fly around in your head and then ricochet through your heart, making your pulse race. These are the problems that most often keep you up at night. We refer to them as your dragons. Why? They breathe fire in your veins. They can find you catching your breath as they arrive totally without any warning. They also often take much longer than you want to subside.

But what if you could engage those dragons by looking at them straight on? You could find yourself with renewed strength. Then you could do something you would never believe you could do: You could kiss your dragons.

Translation? What if you could fall in love with your problems? This is the first pathway you can travel from your head to your heart where you can begin the process of real acceptance.

Let's put this in business terms: The CEO and the senior leadership are afraid of being publicly humiliated. Surprisingly, they're the ones who are most likely to have the greatest resistance to leaning in, to kissing their dragons, their problems or fears. It's scary to lean in. The proverb "The higher you climb the farther you fall" is relevant here. Why? Because you may well believe you are risking your very livelihood. But if you are a leader, this is just what you need to do. This is about becoming a disruptor. You need to hear the call of your dragons. Then address your dragons, embrace them, and kiss them.

Robin: Let's just break it down. When you think about trying to kiss a fire-breathing massive beast, with the biggest-teeth-in-the-world dragon, Shawn jumps in provocatively asking our leaders to become disruptors with the question:

How might you not just address, but kiss, your dragons?

This is a great example of trying to figure out how to fall in love with the undercurrent that lies beneath our greatest fears. Our old way of saying it was Fall in Love with the Problem.

But here's the dilemma: Some leaders might end up going around and around in circles, trying different ways to kiss their dragons (their problems). If they stay with this approach, they will keep circling and spinning. As a result, hopefully, with time, they will figure out, "OK, it's fine if I bend the tail and run around my dragons three times, and then scoot in under their large fearsome chin. Then you can probably kiss your dragons," versus others who may decide, "Nah, I don't want to get burned. I think I'll hide somewhere until it's safe."

For the disruptors, it's all about figuring out how to kiss their dragons by first being willing to address their dragons—those big hairy problems they are facing. The Vikings in *How to Train Your Dragon* are trained to either run from dragons or fight them. That's the mindset side of the pathway. What we're suggesting, though, is to move down the pathway to the heartset where you address, embrace, and just kiss your dragons!

So yes, kissing dragons is definitely a heartset. We're talking about reimagining and embracing the dragons. And remember, dragons aren't those scary creatures that we grew up fearing. This is not for those *Game of Thrones* fans out there where the dragon burned down the whole town. If you take nothing else from our dragon metaphor, we want you to embrace and reframe how you think about dragons.

Has Arianna Huffington Kissed Her Dragons?

Shawn: At age 55, Arianna Huffington started *The Huffington Post*. She turned 70 in July 2020. Influential? No question. Inspirational? Without a doubt. But let's take a deeper dive and examine some of the many ways that Arianna has kissed a few dragons in her day.

We were fortunate to have Arianna as a recent guest on our podcast, *The Combustion Chronicles*. She is an incredibly busy, yet equally gracious and generous individual. Born in Greece, she moved to England when she was 16 years old and went on to graduate from Cambridge University with an M.A. in economics. At age 21, she became president of the highly regarded debating society, the Cambridge Union. You could say that was two dragons for the price of one, or maybe she kissed a two-headed dragon there!

Fast forward to 2005, when she launched *The Huffington Post*, world renowned as one of the internet's most popular, linked to, and often-cited news and blog sites. Mwah! Another dragon kissed.

Then came a huge dragon that resulted from the previous one. In 2012, The Huffington Post received a Pulitzer Prize for national reporting. Score another dragon kiss for Arianna.

Additional achievements include being named on *Time* magazine's list of the world's 100 most influential people, as well as ranking on the *Forbes* Most Powerful Women list. She's got an amazing track record, wouldn't you agree? But as late-night infomercials are so fond of saying, "But wait. There's more!" Sister, is there ever!

Arianna is a best-selling author, with 15 books to her credit, including *Thrive: The Third Metric to Redefining Success and Creating a Life of Well-Being, Wisdom, and Wonder*, which debuted at number one on the *New York Times* best-seller list.

In 2007, Arianna suffered a collapse due to exhaustion and sleep deprivation.[5] Never one to simply lie down and give up (even in the face of physical collapse), her experience awakened a passion within her to explore the link between well-being and performance, which led to her most recent book, *The Sleep Revolution: Transforming Your Life One Night at a Time*, which examines the science, history, and mystery of sleep. She launched a worldwide speaking tour, sharing what she'd learned. It opened her eyes and led her to two significant insights. She realized that on an international level, human beings are experiencing stress and burnout at epidemic levels and that people deeply crave being able to change the way they work and live.

Ready for another dragon, she created Thrive Global, whose mission is to rise above merely raising awareness to creating an effective, real-world tangible solution that assists individuals, companies, and communities to enhance and strengthen their well-being and performance so that they may realize their greatest potential.

As the founder and CEO of Thrive Global, Arianna makes sure that the company's foundational offerings are based upon sustainable, science-based solutions that augment and enhance well-being and performance alike.

An incredible researcher, Arianna's efforts here revealed scientific studies that showed a widespread belief that in order to be successful, you must make the sacrifice of burning yourself out. She and Thrive Global are now teaching others to prioritize well-being over working yourself to death. The results are dramatic, evidenced by studies where decision-making, creativity, and productivity all exponentially improve when well-being is given credence and moved to the top of the list. On her website, she says, "Thrive Global is committed to accelerating the culture shift that allows people to reclaim their lives and move from merely surviving to thriving."

So the three of us, without any reservation whatsoever, classify Arianna Huffington as a world-class dragon kisser and applaud her for all she does to inspire and uplift others to do the same.

Serial Dragon Kissing

 Robin: Arianna is a serial dragon kisser for sure! Her journey reminds me of how nimble Shawn is at shifting from one dragon to the next.

He and I had probably known each other for a few months when I was asked by a friend's company to lead a design thinking session for her and her management team. I told her, "Well, I can't do something like that as an executive of another company, but I'll introduce you to Shawn and make him do it." Shawn countered that with, "Why don't we do it together?"

Shawn and I had a prep meeting of eight minutes . . . maybe.

 Shawn: Eight minutes and two glasses of wine!

 Robin: Yes, and that's rounding down on the wine and rounding up on the time! Anyway, we ran the session the next day and had drinks with the team afterward. They were in awe, gushing with statements like, "This is one of the best things we've ever attended" and "You two are so in sync, you must have years of experience working together."

Shawn and I looked at each other and said, "No, actually we've never done this together before."

I'm telling you this story because the two of us shared such a deep commitment to falling in love with the problem and kissing our dragons, that we didn't—and don't—need a lot of runway.

No matter what we're talking about in the disruption and innovation space, it all comes back to challenging people to identify and embrace whatever challenge is holding them back from making a huge impact in the world.

Sometimes the challenge is a problem that a company is trying to solve in order to fulfill its mission. At other times, the problem ends up being how the company is functioning, which is holding the company back from fulfilling its mission.

 Shawn: So, let's go deeper into that because that's where the messiness comes in.

Michael: Exactly. Too often, the true problem that needs to be embraced (i.e., the true dragon that needs to be kissed) is a personal challenge that an individual is struggling with. Often it's a leader or decision maker who is being held back by a dragon or two and these dragons end up causing trouble for the entire team or the entire organization.

 Shawn: That's where the authenticity has come in. Everyone person in the organization—including the leaders and decision-makers—have to have space to fall in love with the right problems and to kiss their dragons.

Robin: In every corporation I've ever worked for or with, they all talk about authentic leadership. Yet I've observed through the years that only about .001% of leaders are authentic in their corporate environment. It's a rare find, particularly with people of color like myself or anyone who feels different from the company norm.

There's this corporate self that you believe you need to bring into the workplace because you have to make sure that people know you deserve to be there, that your vocabulary is as extensive as everyone else's, that you have that "leadership presence."

But authenticity today is essential for leaders. And this is why finding and kissing your dragons makes so much sense.

Summary

Too often, people jump straight to the solution in business and in life. In fact, in many circles being "solution-focused" is a mark of success. Before you can get to a solution that can actually make a difference, though, you have to fall in love with the problem. More importantly, you have to fall in love with the right problem. It's easy to jump to conclusions and ram your simple, egocentric solution down everyone else's throats instead of doing the hard work of identifying and embracing the specific problem that's causing you trouble.

The mindset of falling in love with the problem leads to the heartset of kissing your dragons, which are the challenges, problems, and doubts that are holding you back. Instead of running away from these dragons that are likely to be causing you some pain and anguish, it's time to lean in and kiss them. But, kissing your dragons is no easy feat. As you stare down all of the troubling thoughts that are flying around in your head, ricocheting through your heart, and making your pulse race, you're going to have to get real about why you were afraid of them in the first place.

Chapter 5

Radical Relationships and Finding Your Dragon Swarm

Shawn: We have a disruptor friend who's a senior vice president of a bank. She told us that for thirty years she had a colleague friend in the banking industry. Over the decades, the two women forged a mutually supportive friendship that helped each of them weather the storms of being female in the world of banking.

A few months ago, when an important conversation erupted around diversity and racism, our VP friend discovered that her colleague friend was a lesbian with a wife and children. It took thirty years for this workplace-based friendship to get to the place where the woman felt comfortable bringing her personal life into her work life.

Here, the question arises, why did that woman not feel comfortable enough showing up as her whole true self? At this point in our world, you'd think that everyone should feel safe and comfortable being who they are. Period. That's where inclusion starts, but where it should lead is combining the mindset of "Radical Relationships" with the heartset we call "Finding Your Dragon Swarm."

Find Your Swarm

We all need people who've got our backs. Imagine what our workplaces, our communities, and our world would look and feel like if we knew we could trust that others were looking out for us. As humans, we're not meant to navigate our lives alone. Introvert or extrovert, we still need human connection.

To continue our dragon metaphor, a group of dragons is called a swarm. If you don't have a swarm, get a swarm.

We've all heard the saying, "Birds of a feather flock together." So, finding other people who have battled and befriended similar dragons (that is, people who understand you and have experienced the same pain) makes sense. Like a lot of other professions, the work of disruption can be lonely. We've learned this. Robin and I both have been chief innovation officers; we all naturally flock together, or, in dragon language, we're a swarm together.

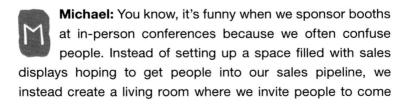 **Michael:** You know, it's funny when we sponsor booths at in-person conferences because we often confuse people. Instead of setting up a space filled with sales displays hoping to get people into our sales pipeline, we instead create a living room where we invite people to come

and just hang out with us. In almost every situation, our booth becomes a safe haven for people to come lick their wounds and talk about all of the things that are holding them back. I can imagine these dragons sitting together, licking each other's wounds and talking, can't you? The point here is that there's no need to go through this alone. Find those who have been there. Go with them and be with them. Have their backs. There's a saying that if you want to go fast, go alone. But if you want to go far, go together. That's your swarm.

Robin: But here's the deal. There's something to be said about birds of different feathers, too. If your swarm looks like you, thinks like you, has the same challenges and same opportunities as you, we're going to challenge you and say, "You don't have your right swarm."

To truly disrupt, you have to surround yourself with people that look, believe, and experience things differently. You have to find people whose values are drastically different than yours. Once you've found those different feathers, embrace them.

Shawn: We recently released a paper within MOFI along with our sister company, Disruptor League (disruptorleague.com), around blowing up the traditional models of traditional diversity and inclusion. Because, when it comes to diversity and inclusion, we can't just keep checking the boxes and pretending like the status quo is acceptable. That's outmoded. Instead, we have to rethink how we approach getting different voices in the room and in our lives. In places that are ripe for disruption, your multiplier will be your force differentiator, which is your diverse swarm of people who will support you *and* challenge you. It's where you'll start to look at better returns, better outcomes, better satisfaction, better services, better thoughts, products, and on and on.

For me, as a corporate pastor, I'm constantly on the phone listening to the needs of my swarm. When they need me, I'm there. I've got their backs. The interesting thing, though, is that more often than not, the needs they have are for their personal versus professional lives. That doesn't matter. In our very connected world, what happens in our private lives often has a dramatic impact on our work lives. My belief is that having someone's back means I'm there beside them without judgment.

The even better news is that after I listen to the people in my swarm, really listen, they feel heard. They are then able to go back to their workplaces and to their home lives, and because they are supported, they are more confident. They are not walking alone anymore. They know they are cared for, even loved unconditionally. That's what really matters. People want to trust others, but first, they need others they know, even if it is just one person, to believe in them.

It's a privilege for me to open up and hold a space for my partners to feel someone is looking out for them and ready to listen to them whenever they have the need to share.

In these very tough times, I know that even a little bit of support goes a long way. So where does this lead? To the swarm!

In the spirit of the swarm, we challenge you to build your community and fill it with like-minded and, more importantly, like-valued people who might be different from you in many ways and have different life experiences and different perspectives, but will always have your back. Just as Hiccup was at first ostracized and ridiculed for his lack of skill in hunting and killing dragons, you may experience similar jabs because you are unlike the others with whom you work or live. But your life, like Hiccup's life, can change at any point when you find at least one person to have a radical relationship with. Just one person can make all the difference. Then, once you have found that one individual that really gets you, you will be on your way to growing your swarm.

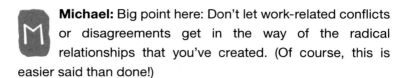 **Michael:** Big point here: Don't let work-related conflicts or disagreements get in the way of the radical relationships that you've created. (Of course, this is easier said than done!)

We talked earlier about melding personal and work relationships and being more authentic in both. Just to drill into this a bit, yes, we want you to blur the line between personal and professional, but we also want you not to let personal relationships get in the way of important business decisions, even if those decisions affect people.

Shawn: Michael and I travel together a lot, which means we've seen each other at our best and worst. People often ask us to tell them stories about our biggest fights, thinking that with two big personalities, surely sparks end up flying every once in a while. It always surprises people to learn that we don't fight. And it surprises them even more to find out that we don't have fights because we choose not to fight. Yep. It's a choice.

Now, we definitely have disagreements. And sometimes those disagreements get a bit elevated. Funnily enough, the worst disagreements always seem to happen when we're sitting next to each other on a plane, which means we're stuck sitting next to each other when both of us would have preferred to walk off and stew a bit. Because we don't have the luxury of stomping off in that moment, we've learned just to sit in the mess together. As we sit there and give ourselves time to calm down, we move away from our own agenda and start to think about the other person's perspective. Then, our minds tend to go into remembering how blessed we are to be in a radical relationship. By the time the plane lands, we'll look at each other and start talking about where we want to go to dinner. Whatever we were in disagreement about is much less important than the relationship, but we both understand that sometimes business decisions have to get made and it's not worth ruining a friendship over.

The metaphor of being stuck sitting on a plane together is actually a great practice for when disagreements happen. As badly as we want to storm off and be upset, the right thing to do in a radical relationship is to fasten our seatbelts and sit in the mess together.

Michael: I'll also mention here that there's some strategy about who to put in the window seat verses the aisle seat. The person who will need the most encouragement to sit in the mess needs to be sitting in the window seat. When you're sitting on the aisle, it's much easier to pop up and stretch to avoid the tough conversation. The person in the window seat, however, is a bit more boxed in.

Shawn: Another piece of this is that as leaders, we have to be able to make tough personnel decisions with people that we have radical relationships with. Even when I need to end a contract with someone on our team, I know that it can be done by leaning into the relationship instead of turning our emotions off. The goal would be to continue a radical relationship even with the contract is over.

This is what having your back and the benefit of a radical relationship is all about. I know this is a clichéd term, but for my swarm I say, "I've always got your back." And by "always," I mean always.

As a result, people in these relationships feel safe to be who they really are and say whatever they want. By the same token, it's crucial that all of us take time to create space for ourselves when necessary. I encourage you to do that now and then. When I find myself with my swarm and I decide to tell them, "I need some space for me," that is a powerful moment.

Finding your dragon swarm means disrupting the way people usually build relationships. Why? Because people very often go for more surface-level connections instead of jumping into the messiness of radical relationships. Michael, as he has shared, is one of those people, and there are more people like him than there are like me. As my publisher, Melissa G Wilson, an expert on networks, told us during our work on this book:

> "My research has shown that most people have networks that are an inch deep and a mile wide. The results show that there are few people who have cultivated deep, lasting relationships that go a mile deep and an inch wide." This latter group are the few, as Malcolm Gladwell substantiates in his bestselling book *The Tipping Point*. These 'few' really know how to build substantial networks of supportive relationships. On the other hand, those who have weaker, more shallow connections spend their time with small talk where little insight or connection occurs."

Summary

Building quality (radical) relationships leads to finding your swarm—that group of individuals that you can go a mile deep with regularly. And though these swarms need to be packed full of people who have similar values and who are like-minded, they also need to include as many or more people who offer a different perspective. Because they're filled with humans, these swarms are not all sunshine and roses. In fact, they're complex, complicated, and messy. In the end, though, these swarms will take us to places that we never imagined and will help light and fuel our inner fires.

Chapter 6

A Bias toward Action and Unleashing Your Inner Fire

 Michael: You, like every human on the planet, have already demonstrated a bias toward action.

Think about it. Have you ever cooked a meal where the pot suddenly started boiling over? You had to quickly respond. Or how about if you were ever driving a car and another driver suddenly veered into your lane? You had to quickly respond or perhaps face getting hurt and doing thousands of dollars of damage to your car. When there's need for it, we jump right in and act. However, if we are not faced with some kind of pressure to act, lots of us will tend to take a slower path on most things in our lives.

 Shawn: I woke up one morning and said to Michael, "We're going to do a podcast." Within three weeks, we'd branded a concept and recorded close to 20 episodes. Yep. We moved from "we hadn't really thought about starting a podcast" to "we've got two seasons in the can" in 21 days.

So, instead of holding an initial discovery meeting one week and assembling a team to take a few weeks to do a feasibility study and then scheduling a report-out meeting with stakeholders to start thinking about making some decisions about a possible concept, we jumped in, figured it out, and made it happen. This means that we had a quick ideation meeting with some key team members who created a first draft of guests that we wanted to invite to be on the podcast.

While a couple of people started reaching out to potential guests, I signed a contract with a podcast producer I liked. We were a full week into booking guests before Michael even had time to figure out what we were going to call our show and what it was going to be about. But, by the time we finished the first round of recording, we'd already created a branding strategy and a marketing strategy and had even created a new website for it.

This undertaking is just one example of a *bias toward action.* What really pleased us with this quick implementation was that we were able to get the same kind of results that other folks get when they take much longer to plan. Even with our quick movement into action, we heard comments from our guests like:

> "This felt very comfortable and intimate."

> "Most of the time on podcasts you have lots of guardrails. But with you, I felt there were no boundaries to our conversation."

"It was challenging but very exciting as I didn't know what to expect, but that was good because it brought up things that were even more special and important to share."

Though we do send some questions in advance to our guests, we let the conversation go where it needs to go, even if that means abandoning the question list. Instead of making the guests uneasy, we've found that they love being in an open, thoughtful, authentic conversation about topics that they're passionate about. And, of course, they know that they can trust us to make them look and sound as good as possible.

A significant aspect of this mindset of a bias toward action is that you have to identify the things (other not-so-helpful mindsets) that slow you down. In our world, these are more dragons for us to connect with. Why waste time on lots of meetings and overthinking a process when you can get the same or better results by quickly finding a starting place and then making something happen? Why invest the precious commodity of time into meetings and waiting when you could be moving the project forward?

Now, to be clear, we're still big fans of due diligence and talking before we jump. The difference here is that the due diligence can happen in much less time than you think it needs. And, in most situations, you could be moving forward with the project while any due diligence and thinking need to happen. Cut your meeting times in half, keep people aligned, and get sh*t done!

Michael: One tool that our team uses to maintain a bias toward action is the 20 Minute Bat Signal rule. Everyone on the team commits to sending up a Bat Signal (a plea for help) if they go more than 20 minutes without making progress on something. The first step is asking for help from people in their work pods and then the next step is asking for help from someone on the leadership team. Instead of worrying about getting in trouble if they appear lost or unable to handle a particular task, we make it a norm to ask for help as quickly as possible.

With time, people understand how to utilize each other's strengths and support each other's weaknesses. And by normalizing the need for help, the team's anxiety levels go down and they're able to move faster together.

Let Your Inner Fire Out

Shawn: Moving from your head to your heart is all about shifting your power from thinking to taking action. Those who can shift to be heart-centered with relative ease grow their heart muscle. And as time goes on, with regular exercising of your heart muscle, you will develop a bias toward action—action for positive change in your life and the lives of those you impact. When people get free and move, it's beautiful to see the results. But again, it's not easy to make this shift. People get paralyzed, actually, when you say to them, "You have no boundaries. You have no limits. Just go create and do and do it fast so we can learn if it's the right way to do it."

In the dragon world, this is about letting your inner fire out.

Annette Logan-Parker

Shawn: Our good friend Annette Logan-Parker, the CEO of Cure 4 the Kids in Las Vegas, which was introduced earlier in this book, knew that she wanted to have a career in healthcare from an early age. When she was 15, she entered a certified nursing assistant program, one of those programs where you get high school credit and the vocational training at the same time. Here's her story, which she shared on our podcast:

Annette: There's a little bit of a funny story, because I started out being a disruptor even way back then, because the criteria to be in the program was you had to be 16 and I was only 15. I just could not wait to get into my academic journey, and so I had to lobby the program, write an essay, and explain to them why I was mature enough.

One of the most important lessons I learned through all of my academic experiences came from my teacher when I was 15, in that tiny, little CNA program. I often tell people, I learned more about how to be a good healthcare provider from CNA than any other program. And I say that because I was super frustrated with an incident that took place in one of my clinical rotations. I won't bore you with all the details of that, but I was going to drop out. I said, "If this is what nursing is, I don't want any part of it."

So, I met my instructor in the hospital cafeteria, and we were eating vanilla pudding when she asked me, "What is it that you want to do? You're 15. Clearly, you're a go-getter. Now you're willing to quit after you worked so hard to get into the program? Talk to me about that." And I just said, "These nurses are so mean, and they're spending so much time fussing and fighting and not taking care of the patients, working against the administration and the hospital that they work for." I just thought, "Wow, like, they're not gonna really get anywhere."

I followed that up by stating, "I want to really change healthcare." So apparently, I knew that when I was 15 years old.

She then said to me, "Annette, if you really want to change the U.S. healthcare system, and how patients receive care, you have two options. One is to complete your nursing education and then go into teaching and teach nurses how to be the best possible nurses that they can be. And then you just replicate that, thousand-fold over generation and generation."

She let that sink in for a minute before adding, "Or your second option is to create an environment where you get to make the policy, you get to write your own rules. And if you can figure out how to get yourself into a situation like that, you will change healthcare, because you will be setting the standards."

All these years later, it's really interesting, because I go back to that conversation all the time and think about how I had to create an environment where I got to make my own rules on what was important in that medical institution. I think that my entire career led up to that, that point in going back to that original conversation when I was a very young girl and reminding me that you either need to educate people on how to be better at what it is they're doing, or you have to create an environment where you make the rules, and then you just make amazing rules.

I think that that's why Cure 4 the Kids is such a unique organization, because we get to make our own rules. Obviously, we are functioning within an accredited healthcare institution, and we have infection control, best standards, and all of those things. But what's great about that is we get to exceed those standards, not just meet them.

Shawn: Yep, Annette is a great example of letting that inner fire come to the surface. To truly have a bias toward action, you have to breathe some fire into all the things that slow you down and hold you back. This is when you have to find your inner fire and unleash it on your fears, your worries, and all of the messages in your head that are holding you back. This is another authentic moment for us where we challenge people to get to the bottom of whatever it is that's slowing them down. Is it imposter syndrome? Anxiety? Unhelpful emotional baggage that you've brought with you on your journey?

Michael: For me, this goes back to the swarm. You have to trust the people in your swarm to help cut through the bullsh*t with you and help you get real about what's holding you back. When you're putting your work out into the world, it's a vulnerable moment. Your livelihood is at stake. Your family's future is at stake. When the pressure gets cranked up, it's much easier to play it safe, which in this case means suppressing your inner fire and being OK with the status quo.

Shawn: The first thing I do when I walk into a room is discern. I may preach the same sermon, but through discerning, the focus is different. The heartset of finding your inner fire begins with finding what is most important to you, and then being authentic about it in the world.

Robin: I know that each of you most definitely has some kind of spark inside of you. It just may not be lit yet. Or, maybe it's lit, but you're not ready to show it to the world.

As a heartset, finding your inner fire is about passion; it's what gets you going. Unfortunately, we sometimes have this perception or belief, or we've been conditioned to think, that we cannot bring our authentic selves to the work environment. That somehow we have to suppress it. I want to talk for a minute about how we can connect with our real passion.

I will tell you right here and now, you are a disruptor waiting to happen. If you disagree, you're likely stuck in some old beliefs, like, "I'm not creative. I'm not innovative. I'm not this or that." I'm calling bullsh*t on all of that. We all have had to hack our world, our lives, in this day and age. We all have had to figure out how to navigate things on the fly. Whether you're cooking dinner and you have a key ingredient missing or you just have to make something work—whatever it may be.

I've gone to people's houses and noticed, "Oh, that's a unique use for paperclips!" We hack every single day, and unfortunately we don't bring that same fire, that authenticity and ingenuity to the work environment.

We're encouraging you to do that.

Daring to Be Different

Robin: A bias toward action is not something that human beings are often comfortable with. We talk about this in terms of finding your inner fire. We know you have your passion; you've dug into it before. Let's start acting on that, and then we can move into a place of being fearless more easily.

Shawn: We once worked with a team who was doing a walkthrough of a consumer experience center with the company's CEO. This was a huge company where most of the employees would never have an opportunity to be in the same room as the CEO.

For this walkthrough, most of the employees present at the walkthrough were dressed up quite a bit. I walked into the meeting wearing a pair of dress shorts and an untucked dress shirt, and on that day I think that my hair was blue. Michael took one look at me and asked, "Are you going to go change?" I said, "I'm not going to change who I am because of the presence of a CEO. I've got nice clothes on just like everyone else."

Even some of our closest stakeholders at the company were like, "Have you lost your mind?" I had several conversations with the CEO that day and toured around with him in my dress shorts and untucked shirt. I certainly did not mean to dress in a disrespectful manner, but I did want to be my true self in that moment.

Something I learned a long time ago is this: If someone puts on their pants the same way I do, then just because they're the CEO of big company, how I dress doesn't matter to me and shouldn't matter to them. This is why this mindset focus is so important to us. I live that mindset. That's just who I am. But I can tell you, Michael's take on that day was totally different!

Michael: Yep. Very different. I was terrified for most of the experience.

Shawn: When someone asks me to describe how I differentiate myself from others, that's kind of hard to put my finger on. I can tell you that when I walk into meetings with CEOs, I walk in usually wearing jeans or shorts. It's what I wear. My hair can be whatever color it happens to be at that time. It doesn't matter. The true difference is that when I open my mouth, I talk straight to them about their business and, though I strive to show as much respect as possible, I'm going to show up as myself.

But if you push me to tell you what the differentiator is, here we go: I don't give a sh*t about what's expected of me or what's proper or what the office norm says. My approach is, "Let's blow sh*t up and let's do what's right for the employees and for the consumers. And if that's not what you want, then we're not the right people for you, and I'm OK with that."

In the last five years, I've made one business decision based purely on finances. As a result, I stayed in a business relationship about three months longer than I should have. It was painfully obvious. People saw it in me. They saw that I was physically and emotionally sick over it. Every time I had to get on a plane to fly to work with this company, it was painful because I knew it was a bad fit. But I stayed with them for financial reasons even though I knew I should have quit. Once I realized how unhealthy the situation was, I called our contact person with that company, told them that it wasn't going to be a good fit moving forward, and gave them a recommendation of who I thought needed to replace us. After that phone call, I felt like the world had been lifted off my shoulders.

So, I don't make business decisions on financial reasons, which scares the sh*t out of Michael and Robin and the rest of our team. It's simply not how I make decisions. I go by my gut and do what I think is right in each moment.

Another way to look at it is that you have to look at your head, heart, and hands. Some people lead with their heads (analyzing everything), others lead with their hearts (going with their gut), and still others lead with their hands (just doing stuff without a strategy or plan). I, of course, lead with my heart.

 Michael: That's true. Shawn leads this way even when it causes trouble down the line. And "trouble" is a loaded word here because it's a relative term. To me, it feels like it's "trouble." To Shawn, it's just creativity in action. He sees it as the necessary messiness that comes when people work together.

In our work, I've had to learn to quit assuming that everyone sees the world the way I see it. If I were completely in charge here, I could show you how to prevent all of the messiness by doing a better job of communicating about everything that's happening before it happens. I would sink time and energy into mitigating the trouble before it gains life and momentum. But I work with a ton of people who are different than me who look at all of this through a different lens. So, that's a dragon for me to kiss. This dragon still makes me a bit uncomfortable, but at least I know how to identify it ahead of time and make friends with it instead of allowing it to make me miserable.

Shawn: I've actually told people, "Don't hire us if you're looking for a pretty PowerPoint deck or if you want to us to disappear for a few days and come back to you with a fully baked solution to all of your problems. That's not who we are. That's not what we do."

Michael: Within the archetype of a traditional thinker, there are big reasons why a bias toward action is bad. If we're being honest, even our own team struggles with giving lip service to this, but not really leaning into it.

A bias toward action is not necessarily about moving fast. That's oversimplifying it. It really means getting honest about all of the reasons (fears) of what is holding you back from making something big happen each and every day. You've got to destroy the "I can't" mindset and replace it with a plan and motivation to move forward quickly in positive ways.

I may be projecting a little bit, but this is what I struggle with the most. And it's because my role is to tap the brakes when necessary to make sure we're doing the level of job that we know we can do. I have to be concerned with quality control every minute of every day.

Shawn: Michael, Robin talks about being "goosey" (aka "goosebumps"). I think I just had a goosey moment there—got little chill bumps. Because to be real, and putting it into our metaphor, you have to breathe fire on those things like "I can't" because it's the perfect example. That's where, as the fire-breathing dragon, you have to actually burn those can'ts. This is the moment where we can use the word "slay." You have to slay that inner dragon, that inner voice that says, "I can't. I won't. This isn't good enough. I'm not good enough." The imposter syndrome plays here, right, Michael?

Michael: Absolutely. And imposter syndrome always catches me off guard when I'm coaching a team member. I see them as gifted, capable, and someone I trust completely to make something happen, but deep down they have a voice telling them that they're not good enough and live in fear of someone figuring it out. It takes a lot of mental and spiritual energy to admit that imposter syndrome is rearing its ugly dragon head. Once I hear it said or figure it out, I change course immediately and work with them to navigate what they're feeling.

But, friends, it still comes back to fear. And, as Robin likes to say, F.E.A.R. can often stand for "False Evidence Appearing Real." It's just our heads and hearts making sh*t up. One of my favorite activities that Robin taught me to utilize as a facilitator involves having a group of people watch two of the group members walk past each other from opposite sides of the room.

As they pass each other, one of the walkers says hello, but the other person doesn't respond. Then, you ask the entire group, "What just happened here?" Inevitably, the group members will say things like,

> "The person who said hello is obviously in a bad mood today."

> "Actually, the other person was being rude to the person who said hello. They didn't make eye contact."

> "Well, I don't think either one of them has a clue how to be friendly."

But here's the kicker: The correct answer to the question about what happened in the scenario is that two people walked past each other and one person said hello to the other person. That's it. That's all that happened. Everything else was made up in people's heads and may or may not be true.

We make up so much sh*t in our heads each and every day. Drives me nuts!

Robin: As we talk about this, you might be coming from a place of heart, but you also have to make sure the people around you know that you're coming from a heart place so they trust your intent. Then you get permission to offer support.

Michael: If you trust the intent of the person, but then their action is incongruent with the intent, do you give them permission? Do you give them grace? What do you do with that? It comes back to relationships, and it comes back to that trust.

Robin: It's important to note that our journey doesn't happen in a bubble, right? It happens with moving forces, counterforces, people who, well, let's just say it, they don't love dragons. They're still in a place where they think that the dragons are evil and must be destroyed. People have a fear of dragons. We have to acknowledge the resistance.

Michael: And if you're coming from a different swarm, how do you begin to let go and trust the new swarm that you find yourself in? How do you learn to trust the people in the process? I think that's part of the journey. Especially if you come from a corporate environment where a bias toward action is not rewarded and, in fact, people lose their jobs because they move too quickly or because they risk putting something out there. A bias toward action doesn't mean just move fast.

Going back to our creation of the podcast so quickly, you can look at that and people say, "Oh, they just moved really fast!" Well, that's part of it. But what did we have to destroy that was in our way? We're talking about embracing a mindset and a heartset where we didn't obsess over certain things. We looked past the stuff that normally holds people back. Instead, we focused on starting with saying *yes* to any possibilities that moved all three of us forward *together*. We were embracing the qualities we held collectively to achieve the best results. And I think reflection time is an important part of the process as long as we don't let that lead us to inaction. That's a piece of it: how to move from inaction to action.

So, what's stopping you?

Is there an antidote? Yes. It's the heartset, which actually involves an action of contemplation, of getting real with yourself, of realizing who you are and what allies you do have in your dragon swarm. And to this end, you must get what you need to create a resolve within yourself to move forward.

There's definitely a destruction here that is the old you dying and the new you rising like a phoenix.

 Shawn: This is the fairytale. Going back to some spiritual stuff and studying dragons previously in my life, the only way to kill a dragon is to penetrate its heart.

 Robin: Whoo! And that's where the armor-bearer comes in!

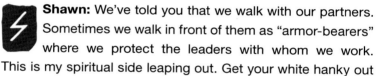 **Shawn:** We've told you that we walk with our partners. Sometimes we walk in front of them as "armor-bearers" where we protect the leaders with whom we work. This is my spiritual side leaping out. Get your white hanky out for a moment.

In the Bible, the armor-bearer was the one who carried the king's shield and weapons.[6] The armor-bearer also supported and amped up protection through diligent prayer. The primary responsibility of the armor-bearer in battle was to protect the ruler behind him. The term armor-bearer evolved in the context of churches to represent those who defend and protect leaders in the midst of the heated conflict of spiritual beliefs.

So, the armor-bearer shields or protects to prevent penetration of the heart. But sometimes you have to kill the flesh. We talked about this in church, depending on where you were raised. And you know, you have to die to the flesh, die to yourself so that other things can live. This is truly where that death and resurrection happens in this heart shift.

That concept of armor-bearer is what gives me the "I don't care what other people think" attitude. This is because I know what I'm called to be. It's innately in me to protect the leader, to protect my radical relationships, and to challenge people to unleash their inner fires in epic ways. Someone may screw me over—and this has happened more than once in my life. Someone once threatened me, physically came across the table at me; but if that person called me today, I would get on a plane and be right there with them if they needed me.

Robin: Saying that "I'll walk in front of you to protect you" is an amazing spin on "I've got your back." It's speaking the truth that accompaniment is really about looking out for people from all sides. It's a holistic take on those radical relationships.

Ask for Help

Michael: For me, this also goes back to the 20 Minute Bat Signal rule. When you find yourself spinning for more than about 20 minutes, you have to be humble and brave enough to call in a lifeline.

In addition to phoning a friend, you have to ask yourself, "Why am I spinning? What sh*t am I making up in my head that's preventing me from doing this?" I think it's the same thing. "What is preventing me from taking this napkin and drawing this out right now? Am I physically tired? Am I emotionally or spiritually tired? Do I need to take a walk? I know this needs to get done, but I'm not motivated to do it."

I had a powerful Bat Signal moment the other day. We were on a morning standup call with our internal team. When it was my turn to go, I mentioned that I have a task that's been on the back burner for me a couple of weeks that has to be top priority the next week or I'm going to be in trouble. Everyone in the meeting nodded and said, "Let us know what you need next week," and I was glad to stop thinking about it.

As the project manager was wrapping up the meeting (which he does very well, by the way), one of our leaders stopped the meeting and said, "Hey everybody, Michael just threw up the Bat Signal. What are we going to do about it?"

I was a bit shocked at this point because I was totally fine with ignoring the task for a few more days. As I stumbled to find a response, the leader looked at me (through the power of Zoom) and said, "Michael, the Bat Signal is real. You need to tell us what you need so we can help you." Within about two minutes I was able to articulate what had seemed incredibly overwhelming in my head, but sounded much simpler once I put it out to the universe. A minute later, my team, who were obviously in a better headspace than me at the moment, had figured out what needed to be done and started volunteering to make it happen. The quick conversation ended with, "We'll have an SFD (sh*tty first draft) for you to see on Monday. Will that work?"

Since you've been reading for a while . . . how many mindsets and heartsets can you identify from that story? A bias toward action? Falling in love with the problem? Engaging your swarm? Most importantly, it's about leaning into those radical relationships.

Even as the leader of the company, my team was able to step up and bail me out when I wasn't ready to admit defeat on making this task happen.

Shawn: Michael, you are really good at noticing those moments. And maybe not in the moment, but you're definitely willing to look back on your life and own those moments in an effort to learn from them so you can change and start moving faster. When you were working full-time in curriculum development you said you just got to a point where you were paralyzed. You couldn't even move forward. But at that moment, you didn't know how to ask for the right help.

Michael: Yep. It was a tough time for me. And, to be fair, the people around me tried their best to help me as much as possible. They were exceptionally good to me and extremely patient. But the truth is that I wasn't in the right headspace at the time. I was paralyzed not just by the work, but the fear of losing my job and everything that came with it. I was afraid of losing the stability, the status, the opportunity to influence, and the relationships that came with this job. It was my entire identity. In the end, the paralysis got the best of me anyway, and I knew I had to leave the job or I would likely be fired because I wasn't producing.

Shawn: You didn't have a swarm, right?

Michael: That's a good call-out. I had a swarm, but I don't know if it was a particularly healthy swarm at the time. I certainly had people I could go knock on their door and ask for help, and I absolutely did. And I would go and say, "I need an activity for this," or whatever. But I wasn't at a place where I could be truly authentic because I was living in fear of losing so much. I ended up covering up for a lot of the emotions and internal struggles that I was fighting. It's those damn dragons, right? I was fighting them instead of being honest and vulnerable with them. I had to learn a hard lesson the hard way instead of leaning into the truth and being OK with wherever the dragons could lead me.

 Shawn: Michael, this goes back to the thing that drives you crazy when people tell me, "I want to come work for you."

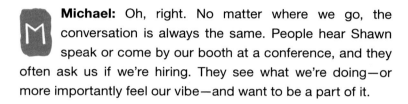 **Michael:** Oh, right. No matter where we go, the conversation is always the same. People hear Shawn speak or come by our booth at a conference, and they often ask us if we're hiring. They see what we're doing—or more importantly feel our vibe—and want to be a part of it.

For the longest time, I just worried that there must not be good employers out there and that everyone must hate their job. Then, I had the realization that people really aren't wanting to jump ship and come work for us. In asking if we're hiring, they're actually just claiming that they're unhappy in their current context and want to learn how to have passion and joy again in the work. They want to actually have some influence, and they're tired of feeling handcuffed and ineffective.

So, we shifted these conversations to focus on how to support people in their current positions instead of telling them that we don't have any open positions. That's why we launched the Disruptor League (disruptorleague.com). It's a space that brings together disruptors, innovators, and change-makers to be a big swarm that supports, inspires, and challenges people to destroy the barriers that are holding them back from making sh*t happen and finding passion and joy in their work. In short, it's building a swarm to challenge people to kiss their dragons, right?

Shawn: Yes. They're trying to find their dragon swarm, the place where they feel the safest, the most supported, and especially the most inspired to change, to grow, to create!

But when you think about yourself as an innovator and disruptor, there are many moments when you're just tired. We all get tired of being the one to always push uphill. We just want to shout, "Oh, my God. Someone just help! How long do I have to fight this battle?" That's the real part, and this is where we come in to help our partners. Why does it have to be such a fight? But I think that's where Michael would say to you, that's where I feel their pain and experience it myself to the point I find myself saying, "My God! I'm tired of fighting this."

Robin: I think there are potentially two sources of conflict. Definitely one is within ourselves, the side of us that doubts, but I'm also trying to think from a dragon perspective. In *Game of Thrones*, the White Walker, the Night King, he's the antagonist. So, in the corporate world, who is the person who is your antagonist? There's always at least one in every organization.

Michael: Back to the movie *How to Train Your Dragon*. The Vikings were the enemies of the dragons . . . until they weren't. Because Hiccup, the young Viking hero in this tale, was brave and, through a lot of hard work and dedication, made friends with his dragon and became a new kind of Viking. He was a disruptor and an innovator.

 Shawn: Right. It goes back to the power you seize by naming your enemies—to name your dragons and, in doing so, step into the role of disruptor.

Michael: Yes. Name those things—those dragons that are stopping you from reaching your full potential.

Robin: This is the walk you should take, up to your mirror, and then . . . name your dragons. In *How to Train Your Dragon*, Hiccup was trying to keep it hidden that he had developed a good relationship with Toothless the dragon. And then, as Hiccup expected, when people saw Toothless, they were terrified, shouting, "Kill it, kill it, kill it!" Hiccup had to show his Viking community they needn't have such fears. He's like, "Look! I can fly a dragon, I can play with the dragon and you can, too, if you'd just get over yourself and try something new." There is the adage, seeing is believing. This relates to the Show, Don't Tell mindset. Yes, dragons are real, and they can be very good partners to help break through our resistance to change, to creation, to innovation and growth.

Shawn: You have to start to show your dragons to think about what Robin was saying with Hiccup and Toothless. Hiccup kept Toothless hidden, but then, all of a sudden, Hiccup's gal pal, Astrid, finds him training Toothless. She is terrified at first. But then Hiccup shows Astrid how special Toothless is by taking her on a ride during a training session. And here is where both Hiccup and Astrid experience the next level of partnerships. They are soaring with the dragon. But more on that later.

Here the heartset truly lives authentically. You have to live and breathe it. And you have to let your heart own it.

To me, it's more than what is often called communication. It's like when Michael made the decision, "I'm all in." When you choose to go *all in*, you find different and better ways of doing things.

And it's moving from just paying lip service to something else—something much deeper, something much BIGGER.

Michael: Exactly. It's taking the excuses off the table. I love the story about Alexander the Great, who sent a clear message to his troops during a conflict with the Persian army. He figured that as long as there were boats in the harbor, his army would always know that there was a way out. If the fighting got bad, it wouldn't be the end of the world because they could sail out of harm's way. So, he destroyed the boats and told his troops that the only way home was to sail away in Persian ships. He needed them to be all in.

When I think of that story, I try to imagine all of the people who stood on the shore (at least in my version of the story) and watched their lifelines disappear. I wonder what they felt as they watched it happen. Panic? Fear? Emptiness? Anger? Empowerment?

I felt all of those things in deciding to go all in. But I was clear that my way out was not an option and I was going to sit in the mess—my mess—and make it work.

Stirring up the C-Suite

Michael: Going "all in" includes speaking truth to power. It's showing not only a different way of working, but also a different way of living. Shawn, you talk about C-suites that were never going to get anywhere unless we stirred them up a bit. This means stirring up both the humans and the structures that they work within. Some of these structures they inherited and some structures they created for themselves. But, let's be honest. If they desire it, they have the ability and the power to change the structures.

Take for example, what happened when you started an internal job at a major health insurance provider. There was a dress code. But you, Shawn, completely ignored it, and you continued to ignore it until, all of a sudden, the dress code was changed. You never had to say anything about changing. You never had to throw a protest. You just decided you weren't going to dress according to the code. You weren't going to change who you were.

And not only did you not get fired, they changed the dress code to be more in line with how you dressed.

Shawn: *How to Train Your Dragon 2* starts out with a whole community of dragons and everything's flipped around. The dragons are no longer the antagonists. The village is living in harmony with these beasts that used to give them nightmares. This is a big deal because, before making peace, the village's entire identity was built around defending itself against dragons. Now that all of their time and energy isn't going into hating these misunderstood beasts, they have a ton of bandwidth to do some amazing things together. Can you imagine this shift from a toxic culture to a positive, forward-thinking culture?

You've trained your dragons, you're in harmony with your dragon, and you're soaring with the dragons, with your swarm — with your unique, diverse, radically related swarm.

> **Ask yourself: What is preventing me from taking action—from tapping into fire and soaring through life? And where the hell is my swarm to make it happen?**

Summary

Living a bias toward action leads to unleashing your inner fire. To make this happen, you have to identify, face, and destroy the mindsets and messages that slow you down and tell you that you're not good enough. You are a disruptor waiting to happen, and it's time to breathe fire on all of the "I can'ts" that may creep into your head and to become the person that you know deep down you want to be. It also means practicing humility and asking for help so that you can keep moving forward. In the end, it's about getting real with yourself, realizing who you are, and discovering what allies you have in your dragon swarm who can accompany you on the journey. So, what's stopping you?

Chapter 7

Show, Don't Tell and *Being* the Dragon

Michael: The Show, Don't Tell mindset is not about writing a letter or making a speech. Rather it's about understanding that it's your actions that change the mindset of others. You can shift people's thinking just by holding space for people to reflect or imagine something different from what they have been thinking or could be thinking.

For example, my pastor friend who identifies as female tells a great story about how she once got on a commercial flight with a female pilot. All the men around her started making all kinds of jokes such as, "We're in trouble. There's a woman driving the plane," and "Women get lost," and all those kinds of easy punches.

Then one of the men quipped, "Are there any pastors on board? Because we're all gonna die." And they did almost die when my pastor friend raised her hand and said, "Yeah, I'm a pastor." That comment shut them all up, very quickly. It never occurred to them that the woman sitting next to them could be a pastor, much less that she'd be offended by their rudeness. That's what I call holding that space. Just by your actions or by your presence, you can shift people's thinking.

Robin: It gets down to experience here for me. The better the experience, the better the chance of getting and keeping customers for life. We're already conditioned as human beings to want to experience things firsthand. Even when we're reading a book, we compliment the author for being able to bring us, the reader, into the story. And we play this movie in our heads about what the characters might look like, the smells that the author is trying to get us to sense, which is why we haven't given you any pictures of actual dragons in this book. (We want you to have your own image of your own dragon in your head!) We all want authentic experience. We value what our eyes see and what our bodies feel, and sometimes we don't have the words to communicate that to others.

In our work, there is the example that we teach where we reference the prototypes that a friend created while working with surgeons. Surgeries were taking longer than they needed to because the surgeons were having to hack their tools to make them better. So our designers worked with the surgeons to create tools.

When the designers got in the room, the surgeons would say things like, "We need something that does this." So, the designers went around and pulled objects together—like a whiteboard eraser, a cap, a clip, and some tape around a pencil—and put the new "tools" into the surgeon's hands. By showing something that even slightly resembled better instruments, the surgeons started saying things like, "Yes. This is more of what we need." From that point, the designers continued to collaborate with the surgeons making tweaks here and there and then left to further develop the tools and put them into production. What resulted ultimately was that the surgeons were able to do more surgeries that didn't take as long, which was great for them, was much better for the patients, and made better sense financially. No need to spend months designing. Just grab some sh*t from around the room and throw something together!

The moral of the story with Show, Don't Tell is around including the people, the audience, the user, whoever has a stake in the experience. And if you want to use business words, it's better to get that sh*tty first draft in the hands of somebody quickly so you can fail for pennies on the dollar than it is to fail on a national, global stage after investing millions or even billions of dollars.

Shawn: As part of the mindset in innovation that says Show, Don't Tell, when I remember being in junior high and high school, the cool kids didn't label themselves cool. They were the cool kids because the rest of the kids in the class labeled the group as "cool." Today, just think of Apple, Samsung, Google, Tesla—so many of them. They don't label themselves as innovative. They don't need to. And why? Because they just do it. They don't go out saying, "I'm cool, I'm innovative." They just get out there.

Not long ago, we had a great conversation with one of our partners in the laboratory space who was frustrated with wasting so much time with new ideas that they were falling behind in the market. We helped them understand that the best way for them to be bold across the industry and in their organization is to get stuff out when it's not perfect. These are our sh*tty first drafts. It basically means you can release something without it being perfect.

I'll give you another example. I'm an iPhone person and always want to have the most recent version. But, when you get the new iPhone, you buy it knowing that there will be some glitches at first. We just live with the glitches and look forward to the updates that will make things better.

If you've been hired to lead change, to lead innovation, to lead design, to lead experience, a small part of your job is to get that done. But I want you to hear me: the larger part of your job is to have people see you getting it done. Let them see you being authentically you. Don't let fear take you down. Don't let "no" take you down. Show it! Show, Don't Tell.

Being the dragon is the next step in the metaphor. You've allowed yourself to accept, to use, to kiss your dragons, aka your challenges. And in doing so you've integrated them. You've consumed your challenges, and in the process they've become sources of wisdom. That wisdom is about understanding that it's your actions that can change the mindsets of others. I got one of the greatest compliments ever from another partner of ours just the other day. We've been with this partner for a little over two years, and this gentleman said to us, "I want you guys to know that you're making a difference because people's minds are changing. It's getting to their hearts."

One of the things we practice is to hold space for people to reflect or imagine something different from what they have had to do or think up until that point. That can be the shift in people's total heartsets and mindsets.

Jason of Beverly Hills

You may not know Jason Arasheben, but you would know him if you saw the jewelry he designs and sells through his store, Jason of Beverly Hills. Here is his kiss-the-dragon story from our podcast:

Jason: I like to push the envelope, but I do it because I want to have a reason to get up in the morning. I want to be inspired each and every day. And quite frankly, if I made the same thing that everyone else makes, life would be boring. For me, it's not necessarily about the money and it never was. It was more about what is gratifying to me as a person, and what was gratifying to me as a person was designing stuff that got me excited to get up in the morning.

So, if I was going to design something, I didn't want to design just the everyday pieces. I remember being a kid and going through my grandmother's jewelry box and seeing some of the items that she had. She had pretty much what you would expect the average person to have. You know, a little diamond necklace, maybe some rings, very traditional pieces. Then I went and looked at some of the jewelry my mother had collected over the years. As I went through her jewelry box, I saw much of the same thing.

So, generation after generation after generation, you really have not seen the big jewelry houses like Harry Winston, Cartier, and Tiffany's really, really venture off the road and off the path because they tend to just basically conform to what they feel that people would like. I decided to do the exact opposite. I didn't care if they would like or not like my items. I wanted to design something that would be fun to make and let the chips fall where they may. You know, if the people like it, they like it.

And if they don't, they don't. But I wasn't going to be satisfied sitting over there just to make a dollar and design something that looks like everyone else's jewelry.

So that's the route I took. I made my first few pieces. Listen, I designed some really eccentric pieces, really awful pieces. A lot of people don't like it. But the people who have liked it have purchased everything. They've gotten everything up and down Rodeo Drive and Madison Avenue and Bond Street and have been to all the traditional jewelry houses, these types of people who are looking for something different.

Celebrities that have seen everything under the sun are looking for something different, something that kind of really exemplifies their personal tastes, their identity, their personality. And my designs allow people to do that, allow people to have fun wearing jewelry again, not just wearing it because that's what you're supposed to wear and that's what's supposed to look good when you go to a wedding.

I designed it for me first. Originally, I didn't know if clients would like it. And when I opened my first store, I was nervous. I wondered, "Are people really going to like the stuff I make?" And lo and behold, they loved it. It was a great reaction.

Shawn: Jason, we met about a year ago. I have fallen deeply in love, and your passion is clear. I want you to share a little bit of a story because I remember walking into your boutique in Las Vegas. I had passed by that door—I don't even know how many times—and didn't even completely understand what it was all about. I even looked in the window and thought, "That's some interesting stuff," but didn't really think twice about it.

I remember, though, walking into your store for the first time, which was the moment that transformed even our journey of how we purchase jewelry. There was a piece there that was custom made after a Disney movie that my wife and I deeply love. And, just so everyone knows, this store is more of a boutique. There's not a ton of inventory on hand and, as I would later learn, the available items change regularly.

The piece that jumped out at me was a pendant that was the balloons and the house from the film *Up*. Michael was with me when that happened, and we both kind of stopped in our tracks when we saw it. We both knew that I'd be buying that piece of jewelry on the spot because the movie *Up* has a special place for my wife and me.

So, what was your story behind building that piece? Because it's exquisite. It's beautiful. And I'll never forget the first night my wife wore it, and where we were.

Jason: Every piece that I make, people always ask me, "What inspires you when you're creating?" And the last thing I'll ever look at it is jewelry, right? It's really about life experiences. And it could be, you know, throughout my travels. It could be looking at architecture. It could be looking at nature. It could be looking at furniture or clothes design.

It could be watching a movie. I get inspired because I love everything that it represents. It's not so much only about the movie itself, it's about the message that it sends out. Like the ascension rising up, rising above, above the negativity, rising above evil. I like the trajectory of it really representing going up, not down, right?

We all want to uplift our lives, uplift ourselves personally, uplift others. The word "up" has such a positive connotation in so many different ways. It inspired me beyond words. It was the message behind it that was the icing on the cake for me. And that is similar to how I make my jewelry. A piece might not speak to the first 5,000 people who walk by my window, but it spoke to you. And that's the real reward behind what I do is that I'll make pieces that might speak to one out of a million people. But you know how much more rewarding that is when I made that one piece that really hit personally for that one person? That's far more rewarding than just making some stud earrings that everyone can make.

Shawn: I think it is important too, Jason, to share that it's not always been easy, either. It's not always been that beautiful *Up* story. There have been some really hard times going against and really disrupting an industry that wasn't always that way. Can you share with us those moments when you wanted to quit or when you felt like you failed, but you kept going? What would you say to the rest of the world as they're starting businesses, or they're disrupting an industry that had never been disrupted?

Jason: I feel like you need to be authentic to yourself, which was what I was speaking about earlier. It is about truly understanding and knowing who you are. That's being authentic. So, when I designed my jewelry, like I said before, I'm not designing for someone else. Each piece is authentic to me. It's what made me happy. Now had I let all the bullsh*t that was around me guide me, discourage me, change my path— money or no money—I wouldn't have been happy.

Shawn: You have to be willing to kiss your dragons. This is about creating and living in a space of faith—the faith that, one day, you will be able to soar with your dragons. I create these spaces at work and at home. For me, creating and living in those spaces of faith is where I collect and build best friends and lasting friendships.

Michael: Yes. We create these spaces for our work partners, such as the time we helped a group of leaders at a major healthcare organization make changes that would dramatically improve their customer experience. We did this by leading a project for them and, in the process of leading the project, teaching the mindset-to-heartset journey, creating and holding a space so the leaders were able to stand up and say things they wouldn't normally feel comfortable saying. From there they found themselves able to buck the system and address things that weren't performing, that weren't delivering the results they wanted and needed. And by holding this space, we were able to help them speak truth to power—even if that didn't mean using words.

We don't *talk* as much about disruption as we *do* disruption. We show each other how disruption can happen. And when you create these spaces where others can move through the mindsets to the heartsets, it's blowing up all that sh*t that gets in your way of creating great experiences.

Shawn: On a recent trip to Las Vegas, my wife (Carla), Michael, and I were attending a charity event for Cure 4 the Kids (started by Annette Logan-Parker, mentioned earlier in the book), which is our heart and passion. That evening, Michael followed his normal M.O. and went to bed at a decent hour so he could get up early, Carla went to the Pai Gow (poker) table, and I, of course, settled in at a craps table.

When I realized I hadn't seen Carla for almost two hours, I left the craps table for a minute to go check on her. It wasn't a big casino, so I walked over and she's sitting in the middle of the table with three guys, who are now all three best friends of ours. Just for the record, this was one of those times where Michael warned me, "No more best friends."

I ended up playing cards late into the night with them. Typical me, I got into a conversation with them that spanned all kinds of topics, and at some point mentioned that I'd written a book called *The Power of YES! in Innovation*. Around 2:00 a.m., we decided that maybe our luck had run out and we headed to bed after exchanging cell phone numbers with our new friends.

Around 4:30 a.m. my phone starts getting texts from one of the guys. He said, "Dude, I'm sitting on my balcony, and I'm halfway through your book. This is life-changing to me." I was puzzled and asked, "What are you talking about? I didn't give you a copy." He said, "I went on Amazon and bought it and started reading it. And I'm not going to go to bed until I finish reading your book."

So, time went on and we built a friendship. Over the months, we've walked alongside these three new friends in ways that have been truly amazing, including flying to meet one of them when he and his wife sadly lost a child to stillbirth.

In that time of developing a relationship, we've also dreamed up ways to work together professionally and know that some incredible things will be happening in the future. Along the journey, we've been able to invite some of them to come see what we do and how we do it. They fell in love with our mindsets and heartsets and are now ready to blow some sh*t up with us.

Michael: That story illustrates the foundation of how we work. We have found that partners want, and rightfully so, authentic relationships with those with whom they work. They want true partnerships where they can go through both personal as well as professional challenges with someone at their side (pastoring) and, when needed, in front of them (armor-bearing). We all need each other and benefit from *not* going through challenges alone. Our partners see the value in these relationships.

Too many people and organizations in the disruption and innovation space are just doing "innovation theater" (meaning they're doing innovation just to check boxes without an actual commitment to getting the results that they want and need).

We're the opposite. This is where the phrase "get sh*t done" comes from. We tell people up front that we're going to move the needle. We also tell them it's going to be painful and messy and we're going to say and do things that push you. And if you want to fire us, we're really OK with that. But if you're serious about doing things differently and better, we're going to come in and we will blow up whatever you need, together. Then we're there for you.

Robin: The way Michael often talks about Shawn beating the hell out of the piano keys, it's basically him calling Shawn out as the bull in a china shop. He's simply not afraid of breaking sh*t. To me, when I listen to Shawn play, it's really beautiful, but I'm a layperson who is just listening to what's happening, whereas Michael, who has more expertise in music, may observe something that isn't technically correct from a trained musician's point of view. I share this because it's a metaphor as to how Shawn shows up. It may not look pretty; it may not fit the mold. But at the end of the day, it's still beautiful music.

Michael: It's *absolutely* beautiful music!

Shawn: But beautiful is a relative term, and it may not be beautiful to everybody. For some people, but not for everybody. That reminds me of one of the health plans I worked with a few years ago.

The board of the health plan was typical in terms of meeting in a boardroom with 24 seats, the men sitting in their gorgeous suits, the women in their beautiful designer ensembles, and an influential executive and I walked in to discover that there were just two seats in the whole room left.

There was one across the table and one right next to the CEO because everyone in the room knows that you don't sit in that seat. That's the seat of honor reserved for the influential guy I was with. But my friend walked across to the other side of the table (away from the CEO) and said to me, "Shawn, why don't you sit next to [the CEO]?" At the time my hair was royal blue, and, no surprise, the CEO was the super-conservative type.

The CEO was well-dressed, put together; his pants were perfectly creased, his shoes were shined, and here came this guy with blue hair who sat down next to him. They wanted to do introductions, and I could see that the CEO didn't know what to do. So, he said to my executive friend, "Well, why don't you start the introductions?" And my friend said, "Well, my name is _____ and I want you to know that I'm the world's biggest Smurf collector. And I brought the biggest Smurf I know today, who is now sitting next to your CEO."

And I said, "Hello, I'm Papa Smurf. Nice to meet you." You can imagine everyone's reaction, but that's the epitome of the people that we work with.

Michael: That's a great example of becoming the dragon that you've identified and kissed. It's one thing to talk about it; it's a whole other thing to fully embody it.

And please let me be the first person to say that this is much easier said than done. Just talking about it is maybe one-third of the battle here. We have to become living testimonies to these mindsets and heartsets before we can actually see any difference in our lives and work.

So, for some of you, embodying all of this may come easily. To the rest of us, it's a gut-wrenching, anxiety-producing experience that we'd much rather avoid. In the end, though, it's just the necessary work that we need to do with the aid of our swarms to be able to get into a new way of existing.

Shawn: At a recent program that Robin and I did, a listener asked the question:

What gets in the way of your ability to disrupt (soar)?

It's been a theme throughout this entire book: It's fear. People get trapped in fear. You have to almost get to, "I don't care if I lose my job; I'm going to do what's right." And I think that is when you unleash that. I remember the point in *How to Train Your Dragon* when Hiccup was having to show his best friend, Astrid, what he'd done with Toothless. Hiccup was afraid when that had to happen, but he did it. And that's when Astrid was able to embrace her dragon. She was able to move forward in what she did—and actually came to change the whole entire Viking community.

One way to bring your authentic self to any organization is to just show up. Be yourself. I know that sounds so simple, but don't let an organization define who you are. Blow up the things that are holding you back and just be you.

Robin: People need to know your intent and to understand your heartset. So how does someone know your heartset? Again, it's by your authenticity. Sure, we all are gifted and have graduated summa cum laude with a bullsh*t degree. We can call it, we can see it, we can smell it. We know when someone is not being authentic. So, if you aren't showing them your authentic self, you aren't letting them see you be a dragon.

Summary

The mindset of Show, Don't Tell and the heartset of Being the Dragon means living and working disruptively by holding space and putting our words into action. It means embracing sh*tty first drafts and doing disruption instead of just talking about it. By Being the Dragon, we're doing the hard work of embodying a powerful, awe-filled way to live and work.

Chapter 8

The Big Three and Soaring with Your Dragons

Shawn: Using the dragons in your life to soar involves lifting off, breaking free. You can't achieve liftoff if the fundamentals are not in place. Want to soar? There are three tenets (we call them the "Big Three") you must meet before you soar. Think of them as your ground crew:

- Do no harm.

- Break rules (not laws).

- Proceed until apprehended.

These three phrases are definitely mindsets, but *soaring*, that's where the heartset comes in. To illustrate soaring, let's look at how a few familiar characters went through the Big Three to soar.

In *How to Train Your Dragon*, Hiccup was an innovator who understood that at his core, no matter what, he should *do no harm*. To this end, he first made friends with Toothless, who was wounded when he first came upon him. Then, following along with the tenet *break no laws*, he put himself into the role of an armor-bearer by breaking with normal convention (but not breaking any laws) to create a device that enabled Toothless to fly again. Finally, he *proceeded until apprehended* by taking a literal leap of faith *and* hopped on his dragon's back in order to help flight become part of Toothless's life once again. This is how they soared together. And this is also how, together, they set examples for the other Vikings and dragons as to how to work cooperatively within their swarm.

And remember, when Hiccup first got on Toothless and tried to fly, it was an epic mess. This is about inviting and involving your swarm in your world: "Do No Harm. Break Rules (not Laws). Proceed until Apprehended." The heartset here is about embracing your fear and saying to yourself: "Let's go! It's time to soar!" Don't sit and worry about it. Because if you sit and worry about it, that's when you'll fail. That's when the fear comes back in, the failure, the risk. That's when all that comes back in.

So we challenge you to embrace the Big Three and start soaring above all of the yuckiness that may be holding you back and telling you that you need to stay on the ground.

Robin: Let's dig in a bit more to the Big Three, though, and look at the Break Rules (not Laws) part of it. Breaking a law almost always involves an orange jumpsuit and/or a big fine or at least a ton of legal fees. And most people have a hard time breaking laws.

Rules, though, are a different story. With rules, we give people permission and encourage them to break or at least bend some rules. Not allowed to have drinks in that meeting? Eh. Bring them anyway. Not supposed to move the furniture around? It's OK. The world won't come to an end if you move that chair. We promise.

Think about these "rules" that guide us each day. Some of them are official rules that have been established and are being enforced by the place where we work or a place that we are visiting. After all, the person who owns the company or location (even a household), gets to make the rules. Before breaking or bending these rules, it's good to think a moment or two about who made the rule and why the rule was made. That'll help you decide whether or not it's worth breaking.

But what about the unofficial rules? The ones that we make up on our own or assume to exist even if they're not written down or enforced anywhere. These are legacy rules or norms that often constrain just because "that's the way we do it." Friends, these are the rules that are ripe for disruption.

Another important note here is that there are occasions where a law needs to be broken to create some "good trouble," as John Lewis always said. For example, there was a period of time where people who look like me weren't allowed the same rights that other folks were allowed to have. By breaking some laws (and accepting the punishment at the time), civil rights leaders were able to move the needle in the journey toward equality.

 Michael: So, we encourage you to break some rules, but please don't break any laws unless there's a really good reason. Of course, breaking rules usually means you have to take some risks, but taking risks in a low fidelity, calculated kind of way counts. That's the sh*tty first draft mentality. However, you do need to take a leap with a bias toward action. Just getting out there, even just showing up, is a good start.

Taking a leap is about not stopping to ask for permission, but taking a risk where you might be apprehended later. This is where you become a dragon yourself. This is where you start breathing fire, rattling cages that others have literally put themselves into. It's about taking strong, focused, positive action.

 Robin: Bill Belichick, the coach of the New England Patriots football team, is known for saying, "Do your job." I love these three words.

Where you are hired to do a job, don't ask for permission. And if you ask for forgiveness, I'm going to kick you upside your head. Just get out there and proceed until apprehended. Meaning, do your job and don't let the world hold you back.

Many of us have been saying something like, "Ask for forgiveness instead of permission" for a while. But you know what? It's time to stop saying it. Why? Because you weren't hired to ask permission. As disruptors, you don't have to ask for permission to do your damn job!

So, while promising to do no harm, why don't you break a few rules by *proceeding until apprehended*? Right those wrongs you were hired to right. When you're able to proceed this way— with confidence—you are truly one with those wrongs, those problems, those dragons. And the only thing left for you to do is . . . soar!

Michael: Let's be clear though. Getting apprehended is part of this mess and part of kissing that dragon. I know this because I'm usually the one who has to do the apprehending. It's funny because in the moment of doing that I often get a puzzled face and more than a little pushback of, "What the hell are you talking about? You told me to proceed until apprehended, and that's what I'm doing. I'm living the mindset you told me to live! Why am I getting in trouble for doing what I'm told?"

And that's when I get to break it to them that, if they're living the full mindset, they have to embrace the being apprehended part. Proceed until apprehended doesn't mean you get to do whatever you want. It means do what your gut and experience are telling you to do and do it boldly. It also means be ready to stop or pivot at any point because being apprehended is always a possibility. Build for it. Prepare for it. Kiss it! (And quit falling in love with your damn solution instead of falling in love with the problem!)

Robin: That is so true, Michael, and this is something that I often struggle with. When I'm on a design project, I'm off to the races. I move fast, create a ton of energy around whatever I'm doing, and pride myself on being a force to be reckoned with.

But, fully embracing this mindset means to also be ready to be apprehended at times, which means being ready to kiss yet another dragon!

Intelligent Disobedience

 Michael: To me, the Big Three and starting to soar all boil down to a term I learned on an airplane a few years ago.

As I was killing time on a long-distance flight, I was looking for a movie, and this documentary came up called *Pick of the Litter*. The name intrigued me, so I started watching it. It ended up being a fantastic documentary that everyone needs to watch. It might even be better than *How to Train Your Dragon* in some ways with regard to what we've been sharing with you.

It tracks the lives of a litter of dogs as they go through training to become guide dogs for people who are visually challenged. While some could end up actually becoming a guide dog, most do not. If they're not cut out to be a guide dog, they either get placed in a loving home to be a pet or they go into the breeding program for bringing new potential guide dogs into the world.

The documentary shows how the trainers teach the dogs how to do their job. The dogs learn how to wear the harness and go forward and backward, turn left and right, sit, and all those kinds of things. In short, they learn how to take orders from their handlers. The next step is what made me jump out of my seat. I think I watched the scene three or four times the first time I saw it. After learning how to take commands, the trainers then teach the dogs when to *ignore* the commands. Think about it. If someone who is visually impaired walks up to a street corner and gives the command to go forward to cross the street, going forward could put everyone into danger if there is traffic.

So, the dog has to be trained to decide when *not* to follow orders. That's called intelligent disobedience, when the animal knows that it's a bad idea to do what they are being told to do.

And the emphasis here is on the "intelligent" part. It's not about spiteful, reactionary, hate-filled disobedience. It's about making an intelligent decision that a rule or norm is not right in the situation and needs to be ignored in the best interest of everyone involved.

In Shawn's world, intelligent disobedience lies in his gut. He knows deep down that it's a bad idea to follow a rule, norm, tradition, or status quo. The whole thing of showing up for work without following the dress code; that was an intelligent disobedience moment and an example of how he chooses to soar.

How might intelligent disobedience contribute to the lift that you need to soar?

Dragons, Pastors, and Guides, Oh My!

 Robin: I just have to bring in another movie to emphasize all of this soaring that we hope and pray you'll soon start doing.

Remember Glinda the Good Witch in *The Wizard of Oz*? What I see here is that Glinda is to Dorothy (in *The Wizard of Oz*) as Toothless is to Hiccup (in *How to Train Your Dragon*). Glinda and Toothless walked alongside Dorothy and Hiccup in radical relationships much like Shawn pastors other people.

With Dorothy, running into that putrid green-faced Wicked Witch and her legion of terrifying flying monkeys, all she wanted to do was to get back home. In fact, that's all she kept saying, again and again, after the monkeys would regularly dive bomb her and the Scarecrow, Lion, and Tin Man, "Help me get back home!" But when Glinda, her great supporter and metaphoric dragon (aka pastor-partner), showed up, Dorothy had a constant caretaker, confidante, and guide to help her make her brave way to the Emerald City to meet with the wizard. Glinda realized just what was really going on with Dorothy very early on.

Then she shows us, the viewers, just how wise she is when all hope appears to be lost when the hot air balloon, Dorothy's ride back home, lifts off without her, stranding her in Oz. But Glinda, with her matter-of-fact fairy angel-like voice trills, "Oh, you silly girl. You've always had the power to get back home. Just click your heels three times and say, 'There's no place like home.'" Yes, it took some time (almost the entire length of the movie) for Dorothy to figure out she could get home all on her own. All she had to do the entire time was just . . . click her heels.

You know what? Just like Dorothy, you already have everything you need inside your head and heart. And you get to choose someone who can be your pastor to walk beside you and point out your path, along with the various potholes along the way. And if you are really lucky, you will locate an armor-bearer who can walk ahead of you and, if needed, protect you. Then you can fill in the rest of your swarm, too!

And again, what about with Hiccup? It's clear at the beginning of How to Train Your Dragon he knew that he wasn't fitting into the Viking world, even though he really wanted the approval of his dad and to make him proud. But when Toothless entered his life, in came a pastor figure who would stand beside him and help him find his purpose.

Finding your pastor guide (or guides!) is about finding your match, that person, animal, or thing that enables you to become all you can be. It's a person who can guide you as you do no harm, break rules (not laws), proceed until apprehended, and disobey intelligently.

With Dorothy, you have the country girl whose growth was ignited by the good witch, her match, Glinda. With Hiccup, a young Viking boy, a crippled dragon named Toothless became his match. When that young Viking boy fixed Toothless's tail that he was also responsible for injuring, it created a bond between boy and dragon that turned a dragon into a friend.

From that beautiful igniting of Hiccup's personal desire to create an artificial tail for his dragon, the two became inseparable. And from their example, a whole community of Vikings followed Hiccup's lead to live and soar with their own dragons in harmony and joy. To add to the fun, the Viking community shifted from being a place where the top entertainment was slaying dragons to it becoming a type of racetrack for dragon races with the Vikings as jockeys.

In each of the above stories the parties were, by nature of the rules of the worlds they lived in, at the very opposite ends of a spectrum that put them at odds with each other, but they needed each other and turned that need into friendship and eventually into partnerships.

So now just to review quickly: We've kissed our dragons. We've found our swarms and our inner fires. And we're getting comfortable with becoming the dragon, allowing ourselves the space to live in faith that we too are wise. Perfect!

Now all we need to do is soar. I will just say, if it worked for Hiccup in *How to Train Your Dragon* and for Dorothy in *The Wizard of Oz,* then it can work for us as well. *Everyone* has the inalienable right to overcome that fear and become comfortable in embracing and finding those moments when *you* can define your own destiny and . . . *soar*!

All dragons—and now you understand that they're problems that can turn into possibilities—look and/or feel scary at first, but when you decide to address them, befriend them, kiss them, and use the strength you receive from addressing them, then you can soar. Anything is possible.

It's Time to Take Action

Michael: Shawn, as he has shared throughout this book, comes by his ministerial approach naturally, but all of us have some ability to mentor, guide, or influence someone else. And it's OK that we all do it a bit differently.

As a pastor, Shawn walks alongside the person who needs some help and meets the person where they are. He'll spend tons of time building the relationship and will stay up late talking to them on the phone. He thrives on walking with people who have unlit pilot lights. He has so much care and patience to offer them. If they're game, he'll help find their inner dragon and help them ignite that pilot light until it turns into a fierce flame!

Robin always ends up being the "mama" of the group. No matter where she's worked or served, people go to her for advice and they're willing to open up quickly. She's able to speak the truth to people, but she's one of those people who's able to do it with a lot of love and humor. And she's filled with a ton of wisdom, so she always has some kind of story or advice that is perfect for the moment. She's also a great cheerleader for people. She's a much better cheerleader than me. She knows how to get a team hyped up when I just want everyone to go nose down and get their job done.

 Robin: Don't sell yourself too short there, Michael. You may not be the biggest cheerleader in the room, but you absolutely know how to get a team motivated. You just do it behind the scenes with a lot of intensity, which can be scary to people who aren't ready for it.

Michael is the mentor/guide who has ridiculously high expectations for you, and he's not afraid to tell you about it. Though he'll push you and challenge you, he's also a natural teacher and will be willing to explain what the expectations are and show you how to meet them. He's that tough teacher in high school or college that pushed you; you didn't always love it at the time, but as you look back, he's the teacher that sticks out as your favorite. He's not going to invest a ton of time on the phone and doesn't love the small talk, but the substance is real, and he knows how to get you to think bigger and aim higher if you're up for it.

Michael: We also love this motto that is not unique to us, which is:

"Never waste a crisis."

It's 2020 as we write this, and our country is in a profound crisis. I believe there are two pandemics happening right now: One definitely is the coronavirus, but there is another one equally as important, which is the social justice crisis. The racial conflicts and injustices that have been present in our country since its founding have once again been exposed in significant ways. What I have seen, and I think it's a beautiful thing quite frankly, is that a number of organizations are taking a position. It's not without backlash, because there are some folks who are saying, "I'm unfollowing you. I'm not gonna buy your products anymore." But for every one of those, there are three others, three or sometimes more, who are saying, "I'm going to purposely do business with you because you're taking a stand."

Shawn: So how do you not waste this crisis? I'm not saying you have to jump in the deep end headfirst like Robin and I do, and then ask in mid-flight if there's water. But what I am suggesting is that now is a great time to practice authenticity. Again, going back to believing that if people understand you "do no harm," they truly understand your heartset and your intent. And then you have permission to take that first step. You have that permission, and I invite you to try it in your next meeting (in-person or video call) around an area where you might have hesitated up until this point.

I love combining our different approaches to being guides with refusing to waste a crisis. It really comes down to empowering people to authentically live into being the guide that they know they can be and to engage the challenges that surround us each day with courage. That's when all of us can truly soar together as a swarm!

Summary

The Big Three—Do No Harm, Break Rules (Not Laws), Proceed until Apprehended—and Intelligent Disobedience lead to soaring. Though none of this may be as easy as it sounds, it's absolutely doable when you have a guide and when you lean into your swarm.

Our challenge to all of you is to take some big steps into figuring who your guide is and how you can be a guide to others while also actively searching for the problems around you that need your attention. Then, let's get out there and soar together!

Chapter 9
How We Soar

 **From All of Us:** Soaring for us is all about our commitment to our "why," which is to right the wrongs in the world by empowering people to transform their lives with courage. That's also why our company, MOFI, exists.

Even though we approach the world in very different ways, the three of us are rooted in similar values that support our "why." We choose to see the world through the lens of problems that are begging to be solved. Seeing problems isn't an act of pessimism. Rather, it's a viewpoint of incredibly deep compassion for the problems that are causing issues for our partners, their employees, their customers, and the world around them. These are the problems we think about constantly and that inspire us. Whether walking beside them in pastor form or walking before them as armor-bearers, we are present, connected, and committed to disrupting the problems that create the status quo in the world.

We do this (our "how") by creating radical relationships, enabling people to find their truth, and living and working authentically as we sniff out and destroy the status quo. Yes, we enable organizations to disrupt their industries, but we know the only way this can happen is if we first inspire the humans in the organization to start seeing their challenges through a new lens.

Through radical relationships, we walk alongside or in front of people (our "who") as they live into new, challenging mindsets and heartsets and, from there, light their own personal dragon flame and breathe their own bold fire to change their organizations and the world for the better.

We don't come with the solutions. Instead, we enable people to blow the sh*t out of the systems, mindsets, and behaviors that give life to the status quo all around them (our "what"). We offer a new way of thinking, a new set of mindsets and heartsets that, with enough work, will transform the way people live and work. And we know that transforming the way people live and work will change influential organizations that will eventually change the world.

To do this work, we tailor our methodology to reach each individual and organization with whom we partner. So, there is no typical engagement, facilitation, coaching, or teaching that we do with anyone. We approach each new partner with fresh eyes and start from scratch figuring out how to meet them where they are so we can take them soaring with us. And, though our methodology (our "how" and our "what") is all over the map, our "why" never budges. We're always laser-focused on righting the wrongs in the world by empowering people to transform their lives with courage. Period.

We start working with our partners knowing their inner dragons are hiding somewhere in their personal and collective DNA. We walk with them as we identify those dragons, and we boldly stand with them as they learn to kiss their dragons. We are there to sit with them as they do the hard work of working through fears, getting real, and finding the fire within their hearts. We ask hard questions, hold up mirrors, create experiences, and provide opportunities to move at breakneck speeds to think bigger and test audacious new ideas. And, along the way, we create messes and show people and organizations how to embrace the messiness that comes with such epic transformation.

We go anywhere, anytime, anyplace. With each engagement, we focus first on caring and leading by example (Show, Don't Tell). As Theodore Roosevelt once said, "People don't care how much you know until they know how much you care."

 Shawn: Now that you've engaged our mindsets and heartsets, it's a good idea to ask your team, "OK, which of the mindsets or heartsets are you focusing on this week?"

If you take all of the mindsets and heartsets at once, it can be overwhelming. There's a ton to dig into here, and it's too much to take in all at once. Even as each of us and our team have embraced these mindsets and heartsets, we've found that over time they evolve and challenge us in new ways and in different contexts. Because of this, we always find ourselves reflecting on specific mindsets on different occasions. It'd be wise for you and your team to do the same.

Here's the one I struggle with the most, so I'm going to actively pursue it.

A powerful scene in the movie *Forrest Gump* occurs when young Jenny and Forrest walked down the dirt road and three bullies showed up. The bullies started throwing rocks at Forrest; one even pinged him in his face. At first, Forrest didn't know what to do and then Jenny, his best friend in the whole world, looked at him and said, "Run, Forrest, run!"

When Forrest began to run, it was not pretty. As a matter of fact, it was downright pitiful. He was running down that dusty dirt road in Greenbow, Alabama, in leg braces with literally nowhere to go. But he didn't give up. He kept running as fast as he could to get away from the bullies. Before you know it, the braces started to break and fall off—much like shackles being removed from a prisoner. FORREST WAS FREE! Not only could he run, he could run fast and he outran his bullies, becoming stronger in the process. Really, you could say he was doing more than just running at that point, he was soaring!

The message in that scene for me is much like many of our experiences in the world. We often find ourselves faced with bullies, sometimes from the outside, but many times from within our walls—the walls created in our minds and, even more importantly, our hearts. We're all afraid of the unknown. We fear that we might mess up or, worse, might fail. But, once we get moving—really moving—we begin to soar through our challenges and see the world from an entirely new perspective.

I'm often asked if there is anything I would do differently in my approach to disruption and innovation. The answer here is that I never focus on regrets, but I do always challenge myself to focus on soaring. I'm always looking for new, creative ways to enable other people to soar. This means finding ways to teach people to get rid of everything that's holding them back (like Forrest's leg braces) so they can learn to kiss their dragons and soar around with their dragons as their authentic selves.

And in the spirit of soaring with my inner dragons I'm here to thank you for walking alongside me and Robin and Michael on this journey. We're grateful for the honor of being in your head and heart throughout the pages of this book.

Aren't books wonderful? They help you soar whenever you wish. All you need to do is just begin. And that's where this book and our stories end, not for good—at least we hope not! But for now, we stop our storytelling, and ask you to take the reins. Jump on your dragon. Soar! And soar! And soar some more!

With our greatest appreciation for you! We walk with you and before you always in our hearts!

Thank you for taking this journey with us. Now that you've completed this part of the journey, it's time to get in touch with us and share your stories of triumph through soaring. Now that you know more than a little about us, we want to get to know you, too. You're a part of our swarm now, and we're ready to join superpowers with you so we can blow some sh*t up together.

Here are a few ways to connect with us and continue this journey together:

Reach Out and
Get the Conversation Started

You can find us by visiting MOFI.co, connecting with us on social media, or sending an email to info@mofi.co.

Facebook: @mofisocial
Instagram: @mofisocial
Twitter: @mofisocial
LinkedIn: MOFI/Shawn Nason

Join the Disruptor League

As a global community of radical relationships, the Disruptor League (fueled by MOFI) brings together innovators and disruptors from as many industries as possible to blow up the status quo. Combining the heart of a tribe and the passion of a community-driven movement, the league ignites disruptive thinking by fostering the exchange of game-changing ideas and resources and by connecting the dots between people's heads, hearts, and hands.

Website: Disruptorleague.com
Facebook: @Disruptorleague
Instagram: @Disruptorleague
Twitter: @Disruptorleague
LinkedIn: Disruptor League

Engage *The Combustion Chronicles* (Our Podcast)

Join the unapologetic Shawn Nason as he connects with fellow disruptors to challenge more status quo in a few minutes than most of us will in a lifetime. When bold leaders fuel big, consumer-centric ideas with courage, vision, and commitment, the result is a game-changing explosion that creates a people-first new normal. Warning: This podcast, which is available wherever you get your podcasts, isn't for the faint of heart.

Website: manonfire.co
Facebook: @manonfiresocial
Twitter: @manonfiresocial
Instagram: @manonfiresocial
YouTube: The Combustion Chronicles

Before You Go

Thanks so much for allowing us to spend time with you as you read this book. We'd like to take just a few more minutes to make a small request.

If you enjoyed this book and gained even just a few insights that were helpful to you, please share them with others. We also invite you to share what you have learned with those inside and outside your family who you believe could benefit from this book.

We also appreciate your rating and review of this book on Amazon, which is where more than two-thirds of all books are sold. We would sincerely welcome the insights you gleaned from reading *Kiss Your Dragons*.

How to Leave a Review?

Just go to Amazon (www.amazon.com), look up this title, *Kiss Your Dragons*. Scroll down to the middle of the page and click on the link (to the left of the page) that reads: Write a Customer Review.

From this review page type in a short review. Even if you have only read a couple of chapters, leaving a review makes all the difference to the success of any book. Your impressions and takeaways truly matter. Reviews make a big difference for both readers and authors.

In our content-packed world, books succeed by the kind, generous time readers take to leave honest reviews. We thank you in advance for this very kind gesture.

About the Authors

What do you call an insanely creative pastor/church musician with a finance degree who ended up in the healthcare industry after a short stint in higher education and now spends his time disrupting things? Well, we're not really sure what *you* call that, but we call him Shawn.

Shawn Nason, founder and CEO of MOFI and the Nason Group ecosystem, lives his life with a commitment to make everyone he meets a part of his family. Armed with the gift of discernment, he has the uncanny ability to walk alongside people as they struggle to connect with their deepest passions and engage their most debilitating demons. He challenges the world around him to be fully present, get real, and knock down the barriers that separate the various compartments in their lives.

Shawn is on a mission to disrupt the status quo by daring changemakers to pour their hearts into their work while doubling down on a commitment to strategy and growth by humanizing the consumer and employee experience. Unwilling to separate his pastor's heart from his work in the business world, he unapologetically challenges leaders to quit the bullsh*t and think more boldly about how to actually improve people's lives.

Like a charismatic revival preacher, he's endlessly searching for the next situation to stir up, inspire, and transform. (If you know of any, please tell him, but you may want to warn the people in the situation first!)

When he's not out causing trouble in the world, Shawn's at home with his wife, daughter, son, and two incredibly lucky dogs. Unless of course he's traveling to Lexington to cheer on his beloved Kentucky Wildcats to win yet another national championship.

Robin Glasco is a transformational, dynamic leader who believes the monotony that exists in most industries is neither sustainable nor desired by consumers. That's why she is utterly obsessed with partnering with anyone who is interested in disrupting the status quo and having a heck of a lot of fun along the way. Robin served at Kaiser Permanente for 17 years, rising to vice president of strategic operations before taking on the role of chief innovation officer at Blue Cross Blue Shield of Massachusetts. More recently, she's been an executive-in-residence and influencer with MOFI and is now senior vice president for key strategic accounts with BioIQ.

As a strategist, she is unable to accept complacency. As an innovator, she is in constant pursuit of annoying problems to solve in new ways. As an entrepreneur, she is bold enough to step out on ambition, yet humble to surround herself with people who fill her many gaps. As a mom and board member of several non-profits, she is protective of the matters of the heart. As a sports fanatic, you'll find her cheering for her beloved Colorado Buffaloes, Los Angeles Lakers, or Pittsburgh Steelers.

Michael Harper's life can best be summed up by his SiriusXM radio dial, where the ESPN channel and the Broadway channel are saved next to each other with the NPR channel close by. He believes in the power of stories and words, whether on a field, on the stage, or in the news.

A big piece of Michael's journey has been collecting and retelling stories as a facilitator, teacher, executive director, choral director, and curriculum designer and editor. The theme that runs through all of his work is a burning passion to create communities of growth that create safe spaces to dig deep together, challenge each other, and give back to the world.

For the past few years, Michael has been hyper-focused on bringing his production, publishing, and facilitation skills into the world of disruption by serving as the chief of radical experiences for MOFI and the Nason Group ecosystem. This means working at breakneck speeds to deliver thought leadership, ethnographic research, and sprint experiences that change people's mindsets and inspire them to shift from bitching about their frustrations to getting some sh*t done.

Michael and his wife, Cheri, are exploring the journey of empty nesting as they dream about new adventures while their daughter is in college. It may even mean that he'll be able to get to some Dallas Cowboys games this year!

References

To learn more about kissing your dragons and to find additional resources, visit us at manonfire.co/kydresources/.

Page 9
1 Rodney D. Archer, "Heartset vs. Mindset." Blog. Accessed August 4, 2020.
http://bit.ly/kissyourdragons1

Page 13
2 Ralph Blum, *The Book of Runes: A Handbook for the Use of an Ancient Oracle: The Viking Runes* (New York: St. Martin's Press, 2008), pp. 139–41.

Page 14
3 Blum, *The Book of Runes*, pp. 131–32.

Page 17
4 Blum, *The Book of Runes*, pp. 125–26.

Page 56
5 Arianna Huffington, "We're on a Mission to Unlock Human Potential," Thrive Global. Accessed July 19, 2020,
https://thriveglobal.com/about/.

Page 84
6 Elizabeth Thompson, "A Pastor's Armor-Bearer Duties," *Career Trend*, December 28, 2018,
http://bit.ly/kissyourdragons2